RE-ENGINEERING'S MISSING INGREDIENT

M ... from was the ... the anniversary of Wales in Maritime
St ... Resources and Econom-
ic ... whose career has also
sp ... legal affairs an ...
ac ... government is delivering
or ... manager and company ...
se ... director of personnel at ...
co ... where he was a director of the
Er ... appointments at ...
nu ... vice-president of
th ...

Ri ... psychology from ...
th ... and is a senior vice-
pr ... Resources International (HRI) of
Pi ... Pittsburgh, Pennsylvania ... HRI is a leading
hu ... missionworldwide ...
in ... Malt Louisiana, Nestle, IK EM, London ...
Nc ... and Royal Bank of Scot-
la ... also for Wales. He has been involved
in ... HRI's new training and development system, including a
learning system for teaching core skills in a re-engineered workplace.
He is the author of a number of acclaimed management books
published in the USA.

developing practice

Other titles in the series

Counselling in the Workplace
Jenny Summerfield and Lyn van Oudtshoorn

The Job Evaluation Handbook
Michael Armstrong and Angela Baron

The Performance Management Handbook
Edited by Mike Walters

The Institute of Personnel and Development is the leading publisher of books and reports for personnel and training professionals and students and for all those concerned with the effective management and development of people at work. For full details of all our titles please telephone the Publishing Department on 0181 263 3387.

RE-ENGINEERING'S MISSING INGREDIENT

The human factor

**Mike Oram and
Richard S Wellins**

INSTITUTE OF PERSONNEL AND DEVELOPMENT

Design by Paperweight
Typeset by Action Typesetting Ltd, Gloucester
Printed in Great Britain by
the Cromwell Press, Wiltshire

British Library Cataloguing in Publication Data
A catalogue record for this book is available from the British
Library

ISBN 0-85292-621-9

1139240 –1

Learning Resources
Centre

INSTITUTE OF PERSONNEL
AND DEVELOPMENT

IPD House, Camp Road, London SW19 4UX
Tel: 0181 971 9000   Fax: 0181 263 3333
Registered office as above. Registered Charity No. 1038333
A company limited by guarantee. Registered in England No. 2931892

CONTENTS

ACKNOWLEDGEMENTS

This book would not have been completed without a lot of work by a lot of people. Large sections of it were contributed by busy people leading major change initiatives. Case-studies on their organisations were written by:

Gordon Steven, a senior executive in the directorate of corporate change at Bass
Helen Bevan, re-engineering programme leader at The Leicester Royal Infirmary National Health Trust
Keith Bater, re-engineeering manager at Rank Xerox
Steve Rick, director of personnel policy and development at the Royal Bank of Scotland.

Much research and writing of the introductory chapter was undertaken in different parts of the globe by:

Tom Falkowski, senior consultant with Development Dimensions International, Bridgeville, PA, USA.

Without the valiant labours of the above-named people in actually delivering imaginative and successful re-engineering, and sharing their experiences, this book could not have been produced. It was truly a team effort.

Our thanks for their valuable contributions go also to the following: Lois Whittaker, general manager of IPD Enterprises Ltd, for kindling the early flames; Judith Tabern, head of publishing at the IPD, for her cheerful encouragement and especially for her restraint in not advising us until afterwards that she had doubts about our ambitious writing time-scale (!); Mike Lewis, a partner with Coopers and Lybrand, who, with the authors and case-study writers, helped to develop the framework for the book; Leslie Willcocks, fellow in information management at Templeton College Oxford, for access to much research material; the IPD library staff for helpful, thorough, and prompt responses to many requests for information; Eileen Shaeffer, PA to Richard Wellins, for outstanding transatlantic communications; Jane Wallace, for efficiently transcribing indistinct tapes dictated on windy hilltops and other unconventional places; Matthew Reisz, the commissioning editor, for gently nudging us and providing helpful suggestions; and last, but certainly not least, Barbara Oram and Ellen Wellins, our wives, for their patience over foregone holidays, weekends and evenings, and for their helpful review of draft versions of the text.

1

THE BROKEN PROMISE – AND PROSPECTS FOR ITS MENDING

☐ Re-engineering is different from other organisational change initiatives.

☐ BPR can promise massive benefits but frequently fails to deliver

☐ Inattention to the human factors is the greatest source of failure.

☐ Success can be enhanced by understanding the pitfalls and learning from best practice.

Re-engineering is a big issue; initiatives are scattered across the corporate landscape. In a survey published in 1994 of 600 American and European companies, over 70 per cent believed they were involved in some form of re-engineering project[1]. A 1995 UK survey found 59 per cent of organisations planning or undertaking business process re-engineering (BPR) activity[2].

Re-engineering's emergence as a corporate phenomenon can be likened to the actor who is proclaimed an 'overnight success'. After spending years learning theory, developing skills and techniques, playing bit parts and going largely unknown, the actor is 'discovered' and gets his big break. Like the actor, re-engineering has been evolving and developing over the years. The concept was first formally identified during the Massa-

chusetts Institute of Technology 'Management in the 1990s'
study conducted from the mid-1980s. Re-engineering,
however, really got its big break when it was 'discovered' by
Michael Hammer[3]. From the incidence of organisations undertaking re-engineering it is clearly thought to be a powerful *maintain*
survival medicine. However, many already consider it to be *I doubt*
another fad soon destined for the graveyard. The rise in scep- *hmm*
ticism is not due to re-engineering's strong potential impact on
process improvement, but rather the degree to which its advo-
cates have been unable to grasp the fact that successful
re-engineering depends essentially on building total workforce
commitment to unprecedented change.

Re-engineering is defined by Hammer and Champy as 'the
fundamental rethinking and radical redesign of business
processes to achieve dramatic improvements in critical,
contemporary measures of performance, such as cost, quality,
service and speed'.[4]

In its purest sense, re-engineering means starting again. It
means:

- wiping the slate clean and beginning anew
- starting from scratch in designing your core business
  processes, not spending months analysing your current
  ones
- pretending that no systems or procedures are in place
- asking, 'if we were recreating this company today, what
  would it look like?'[5]

Typically, a business process re-engineering initiative differs
from other approaches to process management by its exclusive
emphasis on core processes. 'A core process is focused on one
or more of the strategic objectives that determine competitive
success'.[6] Because of the nature of core processes, re-engineering means sweeping change that potentially touches all parts
of an organisation.

There are numerous examples of organisations which have
achieved dramatic results through re-engineering. For example:

- Aetna Life cut the time for issuing automobile insurance
  policies from 30 to two days and halved its costs into the
  bargain.

- American Airlines reduced its inventory by over a third and made substantial improvements in other areas of its business as a result of its re-engineering programme.
- A Lucas Industries' automotive business reduced manufacturing lead times from 55 to 12 days, cut order-to-dispatch lead times from 105 to 32 days, doubled inventory turns, increased productivity by half and reduced floor-space requirements, enabling two factories to be closed.
- Pilkington Optronics has cut manufacturing lead times from 15 to 7 months, raised delivery-to-schedule accuracy from 10 to 97 per cent, cut work in progress (WIP) orders from 9,000 to 900, raised purchasing on-time from 60 to 90 per cent and cut design changes from 3,500 to 2,000.[7]

Results like these are generated by broad, sweeping changes in organisations. It is because of the nature and results of the sweeping change that re-engineering is both so compelling and so difficult. The broad scope of re-engineering brings with it the potential for high rewards.

Many things can trigger the need for re-engineering both outside and inside the organisation. External catalysts include things such as mergers, loss of a key customer, market share loss, rapid environmental changes and deregulation. The need for re-engineering can also be triggered by internal aspects of your organisation such as layered bureaucracies, too much paper, excessive work hand-offs, too much fire-fighting and too many functional silos. Looking at all of these factors, it is easy to get the impression that re-engineering is always triggered by adverse situations. Some re-engineering efforts are initiated by those organisations that are on top and want to stay there. Whatever the reason, re-engineering and its promise of radical improvements have captured the minds and hearts of business leaders around the globe.

Successful re-engineering – fact or fiction?

Re-engineering is a high-stakes proposition which combines core processes and people at an organisation-wide level. It has received as much press for its failures as it has for its successes. Failure, in conjunction with re-engineering, is often defined as the 'inability to meet the high expectations'.[8] Using this definition, many re-engineering efforts generate results, just not the magnitude of results initially hoped for by the organisation. Estimates of the number of 'failures' ranges to as high as 70 or 80 per cent of all initiatives. Whether or not failures are that high, the majority of re-engineering initiatives almost certainly do not succeed in the way hoped for. Hammer and Champy estimated that 'between 50 per cent and 70 per cent of reengineering efforts are not successful in achieving the desired breakthrough performance'.[9] If the majority of organisations are undertaking or thinking about BPR (as the surveys earlier quoted suggest) then the implications for those organisations are considerable. They must take notice of the reasons for shortfall.

Much has been written on the numerous reasons for failure associated with re-engineering. The failures can be 'caused by trying to do too much, by not appreciating the risk factors (communications, measures, accountability), and by not putting good people on the project'.[10] In addition, there are many other risk factors that include taking the wrong 'medicine', going too fast (or too slow), stopping mid-stream, insufficient up-front planning, overemphasis on information technology, etc.

Of all the potential risks, we believe that the biggest cause of failure is a 'missing ingredient'. More often that not, re-engineers pay exclusive attention to information technology (IT) and process redesign breakthroughs. These may be fundamental but, in reality, these constitute only part of the recipe for success. The human factor is the vital missing ingredient.

A UK report based on extensive research shows that the top barrier to successful re-engineering is 'managing change'.[11] The people-related issue of 'culture' has been shown to be the major inhibitor to re-engineering progress among US and European organisations.[12] Another UK source highlights that people issues featured in four of the top five barriers identified, the first and most significant barrier being 'middle management resistance'.[13] The other people-related barriers in the top five were (in descending order) 'top/senior management support', 'the prevailing culture and political structure' and 'employee fear and resistance'. Given that executives are usually the instigators of re-engineering and always the managers of it, but that top and middle management seem to be the most significant people-related barriers to its success, this is clearly a fundamental people problem. Out of nine critical success factors, six were related to human and political issues. The collective response, when respondents to the survey were asked what they had learned from their BPR experiences, was summarised as 'pay much earlier, focused attention to the human and political issues inherent in BPR'.

The *missing ingredient*, and ultimate key to successful re-engineering, is the human factor in managing fundamental organisational change. Managing change is all about people! It is this missing ingredient that has led to re-engineering's broken promise of dramatic results and well-publicised failures.

All re-engineering organisations need to focus on operational processes and technology. Most will be influenced by their market-places and some will be influenced by other external factors such as government intervention or influence. Figure 1.1 illustrates internal and external influences interacting upon 'physical' and 'behavioural' issues.[14] In order to transform an organisation appropriately, all four of the indicated quadrants need to be satisfied. The quadrant most frequently given inadequate attention or omitted, re-engineering's missing ingredient, is represented by the shaded area.

Figure 1.1

THE MISSING INGREDIENT

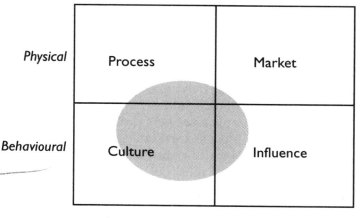

	Process	Market
Physical		
Behavioural	Culture	Influence
	Internal	*External*

An information technology source based upon widespread research concludes: 'change management needs to be put at the core of BPR activity' and highlights the need for 'dealing with, rather than marginalising human, social and political issues'.[15]

The case for attention to the human factor in re-engineering is neatly summarised in one perspective, 'it is not BPR's inflated sense of novelty so much as its shallow, technicist appreciation of the human dimension of organisational change that renders it vulnerable to failure and must be addressed, not least by HRM specialists'.[16]

This book, *Re-engineering's Missing Ingredient*, is all about the 'human' side of re-engineering. Through case studies, we will highlight the ways in which organisations have addressed the missing ingredient. The organisations who offered their stories for this book have looked at re-engineering from a total perspective including the needs arising from their markets and other external influences, and the internal aspects of process redesign, technology and effective change management.

People are barriers – not processes

Let's take a closer look at some of the organisational change and people barriers that hinder the process of re-engineering. 'At the heart of re-engineering is the notion of discontinuous thinking – of recognizing and breaking away from outdated rules and fundamental assumptions that underlie operations'.[17] Applying discontinuous thinking to the redesign of core processes is what gives re-engineering the power to generate radical break-throughs. It is also the source of a vast number of the barriers. To re-emphasise, most barriers do not stem from the inability technically to redesign core processes across the entire business enterprise – while definitely not easy, that's relatively the easiest part. The difficulty stems from the dramatic changes that are required to implement new processes. 'A radical change in the structure of a process inevitably entails dramatic change in all other aspects of the organization which includes the content and definition of jobs, the shape of the organizational structure, and the values and beliefs that people have about what is important to the organization.'[18]

These changes inevitably precipitate 'people barriers'. The

missing ingredient – the organisational/human resources changes – lies in effective change management that addresses the people barriers. Don't underestimate the importance or difficulty associated with managing change. Through our own experience and research we've identified numerous human resource barriers that are not being sufficiently addressed to manage successfully the large-scale change which accompanies re-engineering. These barriers and associated solutions are given in Table 1.1

Table 1.1

BPR DELIVERY BARRIERS AND INDICATIVE SOLUTIONS

Barrier		Solution
Inadequate leadership	➜	New roles and behaviours
Insufficient communication	➜	Personal and organisational communications
Inappropriate structures	➜	Empowered teams
Inadequate preparation for new roles	➜	Role clarity and training
Misaligned systems	➜	Redesign of selection, performance management and reward systems

Inadequate leadership

Perhaps the most critical piece to the success of re-engineering is courageous leadership, leadership that is able to drive widespread changes across the entire organisation. This is especially challenging because re-engineering may mean that senior leadership could be tasked with dismantling organisational structures that they helped to create, convincing other senior managers to go back to point zero, potentially losing stature in the organisation and go against the very assumptions which helped to make their organisation successful in the first place. In the midst of all of this uncertainty, they must create a sense of urgency and quick wins to keep the effort on track. The magnitude of these tasks can easily expose weak leadership and uncover chinks in their armour never before noticed. The importance of leadership was revealed by a detailed research analysis conducted with 20 organisations in the midst of re-engineering. Of these organisations, only five achieved their projected impact. In four out of five of these successes, new chief executives had to be brought in before or during the projects. These were senior executives who understood how to lead an organisation through a period of radical change by combining a tenacious pursuit of performance objectives with a flair for building consensus at all organisational levels.[19] This is not to say that you need new leadership to re-engineer successfully. It does, though, highlight the fact that many CEOs 'either don't have the courage – or see the need – to throw away everything they've had a hand in creating'.[20]

The need for leadership transformation is not limited to top levels. In a study of evolving leadership practices, Howard and Wellins identified new roles and approaches for high-involvement leadership at all levels.[21]

Insufficient communication

It's impossible to communicate too much during a dramatic change process like re-engineering. Yet some people have mistakenly seen re-engineering as a return to the days of old, or the 'autocrat's salvation'.[22] Re-engineering should not mean that decisions are once again secretly made in smoke-filled rooms and information made privy to only a small handful of people. Communication in all directions is key throughout the entire re-engineering process. Used effectively, communication can help to minimise other barriers to re-engineering. From early on when the decision is first made to embark upon a re-engineering effort, and throughout the entire implementation, open and frequent communication is critical.

Employees are typically sceptical about any new initiative. In fact, in an Ernst and Young survey conducted in the UK, '23 of 27 companies reported that the biggest challenge is to convince employees that change is necessary and to obtain their commitment to the programme'.[23] Failing to create and communicate strong links between your re-engineering initiatives and your overall corporate strategy (vision, values, critical success factors) will only heighten their scepticism. Part of the success of re-engineering will be the ability to develop and communicate a compelling case for change within the organisation. This case for change should be linked with the internal and external factors driving an organisation towards change.

As Figure 1.2 illustrates, communications can come from multiple sources. Multiple channels need to be used to get the word out to everyone involved in the change. Formal communications (eg newsletters, videos, speeches) should be reinforced with informal communication, such as face-to-face discussions about the implementation and its potential. Communication plans should also take into account the target audience. One method or message will not quell everyone's concerns and fears.

Figure 1.2

ILLUSTRATIVE METHODS OF COMMUNICATION

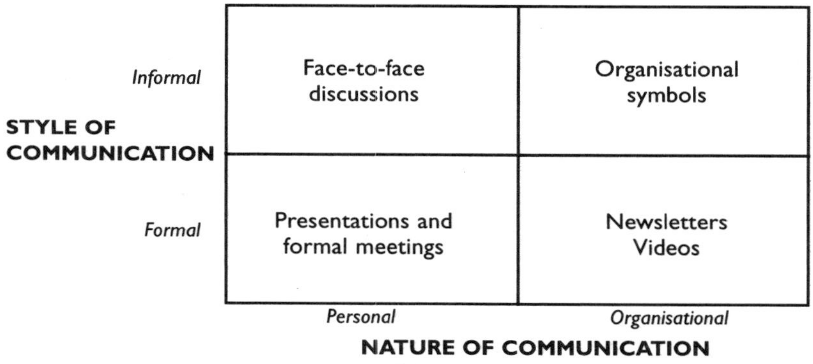

	Personal	Organisational
Informal	Face-to-face discussions	Organisational symbols
Formal	Presentations and formal meetings	Newsletters Videos

STYLE OF COMMUNICATION

NATURE OF COMMUNICATION

Inappropriate structures

Another important barrier to the success of re-engineering is trying to make a new process work in an organisation structure filled with functional barriers, multiple levels and 'silos'. In implementing a re-engineering solution, organisations fail to address adequately the depth of the change. The process must penetrate to the company's core, fundamentally changing six crucial organisational elements or depth levers: roles and responsibilities, measures and incentives, organisational structure, information technology, shared values, and skills'.[24] All of these factors must be adequately addressed to ensure success. One of the most difficult to address is that of structure.

Re-engineering is essentially a team-based activity. Trying to implement teams in an organisation designed for individuals is a difficult and risky proposition. To gain a better understanding of why it is so difficult to implement teams, yet so critical to re-engineering, it is helpful to go back to the very roots of modern-day organisations, Frederick Winslow Taylor and scientific management. Taylorism advocated that to gain optimal efficiencies, tasks needed to be broken down into their smallest component, then standardised across the entire system of manufacturing. This way unskilled workers could become more productive than the same number of skilled craftsmen.

These concepts with the standardisation of parts were at the heart of mass production and central to the industrial revolution. The bulk of business practice throughout the twentieth century has been built on the foundation of the components articulated by Taylor. However, the concepts failed to take into account two important factors. First, it's difficult to force fit people into narrowly defined jobs and remove all human elements. Second, mass production is unable to accommodate today's consumer needs, which call for flexibility, short runs and frequent changes. Re-engineering accounts for both of these factors, often through the use of teams.

The fact that these concepts are so ingrained into today's managers and decision makers makes the task of moving to a team-based organisation difficult. Problems occur: 'when organizations are structured around functional "silos", having dozens of individual job classifications, [and] require a multitude of hand-offs among departments in order to complete a product or deliver a service. In such organizations, it becomes almost impossible to provide the authority, responsibility, and sense of ownership necessary for empowered teams'.[25]

Effective implementation of re-engineered processes in a team-based environment requires careful redesign of organisational structures using techniques which not only look at the technical redesign aspects, but also the social and human aspects.

Inadequate preparation for new roles

Unclear roles and responsibilities can be a significant barrier to the success of re-engineering. We've already discussed the new roles of leadership, but the change doesn't stop with leaders. People throughout the organisation will be called on to fill new roles, acquire new skills and change their behaviour. 'Individual behavior is shaped by the roles that people play in the organization. Thus, the most effective way to change behavior is to put people into new roles in the organization which would impose new relationships on them. This creates a situation that forces new attitudes and behaviors to emerge in people.'[26]

Clearly, establishing roles and expectations early in the process can not only help you to achieve the change you desire, it's a vital part in ensuring the success of the new process as well as individuals working in the process.

It is highly likely that the new 're-engineered' organisation will require employees that are flexible and can adapt readily to changes. This does not mean that the specifics of the new role should be left to chance. As part of the design, and prior to implementation, the new roles and responsibilities of leaders and employees should be identified and analysed, along with the skills and motivations that will be required to fill these new roles successfully. Training and particularly learning become big factors in helping employees at all levels adapt to their new roles. Multi-skilling, often an outcome of the re-engineered process, can require extensive training in new technical skills. However, learning must go far beyond technical and business skills. In challenging existing paradigms and conventions, re-engineering puts decisions in the hands of the people who actually do the work. This higher level of autonomy means that leaders and associates alike must be better coaches, communicators and 'people problem solvers'. Greater levels of customer contact require skills in routine customer interactions. Basic business knowledge and understanding are also a must.

We've talked about the important role that teams play in re-engineering, and the fact that successful teams just don't happen because you put people together and call them a team. Operating in teams requires skills for leading meetings, reaching consensus, and valuing diversity. At the very least, teams which do not develop these skills will never reach their full potential. In the worst-case scenario, teams without adequate skills will fail miserably even in the attempted accomplishment of the simplest of tasks.

One final, yet critical, area of skill development needed for associates in the re-engineered work environment is the ability to promote trust in the work environment. Re-engineering dramatically changes or eliminates the traditional environment, hierarchies and functional silos in organisations. Historically, many of these hierarchies were put into place because of distrust in the workplace. Systems and procedures were established to create multiple checks and balances which maintained tight control over all operations and little autonomy in the workplace. Changing this traditional environment without building an atmosphere of trust is tantamount to disaster.

Misaligned systems

Organisational systems have a dramatic impact in the way they drive individual and group behaviour. Many re-engineering efforts fail adequately to consider the behaviours which their current systems are encouraging, or inhibiting. Any re-engineering effort should include a comprehensive review of all relevant systems strategies for realigning those systems which contradict organisational goals.

While all systems are important, there are five groups of systems that are critical to the ongoing success of re-engineering effort. These are people resourcing systems, including role definition, resource planning, selection and release from the organisation, reward systems including non-monetary as well as monetary rewards, training and development systems, employee relations systems including communications systems and representation systems, and systems for management of people, such as performance management. Of these, three are universally critical to the successful delivery of business process re-engineering:

☐ selection
☐ performance management
☐ rewards/compensation.

It has been pointed out, that: 'Associates in a reengineered company require a different set of job skills and motivations than those in a traditional organization. This can necessitate going through a process of identifying new job competencies for newly designed jobs and revising selection and promotion systems that reflect those competencies.'[27] Traditional selection and promotion systems and tools simply do a poor job or provide invalid data on job dimensions such as teamwork, problem solving ability, coaching and service orientation.

Another system which is crucial to the success of re-engineering is performance management. Effective performance management systems can impact upon re-engineering in two critical ways. First, they create strategic focus by driving an organisation's vision, critical success factors and values throughout all levels and departments. Second, a sound performance measurement system can ensure people better understand their new roles and responsibilities. Performance management can be one of the most powerful change levers available to re-engineers. Yet its role in managing change is often totally overlooked.

The last system which is critical to re-engineering delivery is that of rewards/compensation. Rewards systems 'should be driven by the basic organizational design and the management style of the organization, which in turn should be strongly influenced by the organization's strategy'.[28] Since re-engineering dramatically alters the design and potentially the management style of an organisation, the reward system must also be redesigned if it is going to be a key driver or supporter of change, rather than a barrier. 'The reward system in combination with the organization's design drives the performance of the organization because it influences critical individual and organizational behaviors.'[29] Reward system changes that are typical in re-engineering include a stronger focus on 'pay for performance', learning or cross-training incentives and team/gain sharing bonuses. The major theme here is to move away from rewards as entitlement to rewards based upon value, performance and teamwork.

Helping you successfully re-engineer

Re-engineering's Missing Ingredient is targeted at four groups of readers: (1) chief executives who will have ultimate accountability for the outcome of a BPR initiative, (2) re-engineering implementation leaders and team members, (3) line and functional managers, and (4) personnel and development/HRM professionals.

Through reading this book, chief executives will become

more aware of the business risks and issues, including certain critical ones, involved in attempting wholesale change. It should also cause them to rethink and challenge the way human resources need to be managed within their organisation in order that people may best contribute to organisational performance within at least the medium term.

Re-engineering leaders and team members will find the book particularly useful as they go about implementing their own roll-out. Valuable information on developing a shared vision, gaining top-down organisational commitment, bringing together design teams, aligning organisational systems and overcoming implementation barriers will help those involved in the day-to-day work of re-engineering to keep on course. They should view this book as a best practices route-map and an encyclopaedia of 'lessons learned'.

Line and functional managers will find the book highly valuable. They will learn about fundamental re-engineering principles, clearly understand the difference between a functional and process orientation, and begin to get in touch with the major behavioural and style changes that they will need to make to ensure the success of re-engineering in their own organisation. Perhaps most important, will be the realisation that while the role of a manager must shift towards the heart of re-engineering and 'letting go', the role of leadership becomes more, not less important. It will be the line managers who model and reinforce their organisation's new values, build and maintain highly empowered teams and serve as owners or guardians of newly formed, cross-functional processes.

Our fourth and vital group of readers are the personnel and development/HRM professionals. Re-engineering's missing ingredient is, after all, about the effective management of those who must live in the midst and the aftermath of re-engineering – our organisations' employees. Unfortunately, not only are 'people' often neglected as the most critical part of the re-engineering equation, but those responsible for developing and maintaining our employee support systems are often left out of re-engineering planning, design and key elements of implementation. By reading this book, HR professionals will learn more about what re-engineering is all about and what they must do in order to be able to play their critical role. More importantly, they will realise that for ongoing success, at the very foundation of successful re-engineering must be radical change of all the processes and systems that are within their province – from first defining new job roles to selection, performance management, reward, relations and release of people from the organisation. *Re-engineering's Missing Ingredient* is a first step to new awareness and development of the sensitivities and requisite knowledge and behaviours that HR professionals must gain and master to become true partners in their organisation during and after re-engineering.

A route-map for this book

Re-engineering's Missing Ingredient is based on case studies in five organisations well into or beyond their implementations: Royal Bank of Scotland, Toshiba, Bass Taverns, Rank Xerox and The Leicester Royal Infirmary. Brief background information on each of the case study organisations is presented in the final part of this chapter. Our case studies purposefully represent a mix of various industrial sectors: healthcare, retail hospitality, manufacturing, service and financial services. The different stages that the case study organisations are at give useful pointers to the management of the aftermath of re-engineering, to managing the continuum and sustaining gained improvements in performance.

We chose to base the book on a case study approach for several reasons:

☐ Theoretical articles and books on the topic of re-engineering abound. Yet another re-engineering dissertation will not best serve the needs of busy professionals.

☐ Many organisations just embarking on re-engineering are looking for a convenient way to benchmark. They want to know what other organisations have been doing so they can plan their re-engineering journey accordingly. Our case study approach provides answers to two key questions universally asked by those about to get started with re-engineering: 'What are the best practices that we should be sure to incorporate in our own implementation plan?' and 'What barriers or pitfalls might we encounter along the way, and how can we overcome them?'

□ Finally, hundreds of UK organisations and thousands of
    organisations world-wide are in the midst of their re-engi-
    neering efforts – long beyond the pilot or introductory
    phases. For these organisations, our case overviews will
    provide some affirmation, such as 'We are going in the right
    direction!' coupled with some consolation, 'So they ran into
    that problem as well!'

More importantly, however, we hope our readers who are well
along in their implementations will receive enough valuable
information and guidance to keep on course or, if necessary, get
back on track.

Unlike other case-based books, we have chosen not to structure *Re-engineering's Missing Ingredient* by each of our five
case organisations. In other words, you won't find all the information on Royal Bank of Scotland in one chapter, Toshiba in
another chapter, etc. We felt it would be far more valuable to
organise the case information by nine essential topics or
success factors. This structure will allow you to read through
the entire book and/or select those topics most relevant to your
needs at a particular time. We have identified eight factors
which are necessary to be managed correctly. These, together
with an overview of 'universal lessons' are described briefly.
Table 1.2 was prepared to help you connect each of the nine
topics to the major barriers introduced in the previous section
of this chapter. Each subsequent chapter will introduce the
topics in more detail and contain information from all five
cases.

Let's take a quick 'walk' through each chapter. Chapter 2 is
entitled 'Getting Started – and what should stop you starting'.
Here we will deal with the initial impetus for re-engineering as
well as some of the factors that should be considered long
before you begin to plan your implementation. Some of the
topics covered include developing a shared vision, gaining
senior management commitment and tying re-engineering to
overall corporate strategy. In Chapter 3 we deal with 'Bringing
the Team Together – Vital Selection'. Here we will cover who
should be selected for implementation teams, the role/respon-
sibilities of the re-engineer project leader and conditions under
which consulting support may be useful. Chapter 4 covers

Table 1.2

RE-ENGINEERING'S MATRIX OF BARRIERS AND SUCCESS FACTORS

Case study issues and success factors	Re-engineering's human resource barriers				
	Inadequate leadership	Insufficient communication	Inappropriate structures	Inadequate new role preparation	Misaligned systems
Getting started	✓	✓			
Bringing the BPR teams together	✓		✓	✓	✓
Preparing and moving forward	✓	✓	✓	✓	✓
Coping with distractions	✓	✓		✓	✓
Fundamental change for managers and management	✓	✓	✓	✓	
Managing rewards		✓		✓	✓
Maintaining morale and momentum	✓	✓	✓	✓	
Managing the aftermath	✓	✓	✓	✓	✓
Universal lessons and postscripts	✓	✓	✓	✓	✓

'Preparing and Moving Forward'. Preparing people for change, dealing with sceptics and cynics, and the role of including external and internal influences are covered in Chapter 5, 'Coping with distractions'. Also discussed in this chapter is the relationship between re-engineering and other organisational change initiatives, which are being done simultaneously in some companies.

'Fundamental Change for Managers and Management' is the focus of Chapter 6. Here, we cover a whole range of critical issues including the role of leaders in a re-engineered workplace, turning managers into coaches and the concept of empowerment and empowered teams. Chapter 7 deals with 'Managing Rewards', covering the options and potential changes that need to be made to all forms of conventional and less conventional compensation and recognition schemes in order to drive or support rather than hinder successful re-engineering.

As we mentioned earlier, many re-engineering efforts start out strongly, only to fizzle out as time progresses. Other companies march blindly on oblivious to the needs, concern and pain of their workforce. Chapter 8, 'Managing Morale and Momentum', deals with a series of actions our case organisations have taken to build commitment and involvement. Examples include ongoing and targeted communication, sharing vision and dealing with both casualties and survivors. Chapter 9, 'Managing the Aftermath', focuses on what needs to be done after re-engineering, including human resource planning, connecting re-engineering to ongoing continuous or incremental improvement efforts and celebrating success. Our last chapter, Chapter 10, 'Universal Lessons and Essential Postscripts', ties all the chapters together. In this chapter we summarise, from lessons learned, the essentials for making re-engineering happen ... successfully.

The case study organisations

To orientate you better to our cases, we give below some brief information on each of our participating organisations.

Bass Taverns

Part of Bass plc, one of Britain's largest brewers, Bass Taverns operate some 4,000 retail hospitality outlets (pubs, bars and restaurants) throughout the UK. They employ 38,000 people in a business characterised by millions of small transactions. In the early 1990s, against a difficult and fiercely competitive brewing industry background, Bass were required, through Government intervention in the industry, to divest themselves of nearly half of their then 7,500 pubs. The retail side of the business was in a difficult and, in parts, declining market and losing money, was being forcibly halved in size and was the least popular part of Bass in which to be employed. Now it is buoyant, vibrant and growing, and one of the most desired parts of the Bass organisation for aspiring employees, generating £200m in profit. A competitor has observed that Bass now 'do a thousand things, one per cent better than most of us'.

The Leicester Royal Infirmary National Health Trust (LRI)

One of Europe's largest teaching hospitals, with 1,100 beds and employing more than 4,000 people. It was until recently, before gaining its semi-independent Trust status, part of a tightly controlled National Health Service bureaucracy, owing its ways, means and many of its attitudes to a nationalised infrastructure evolved over 50 years. Hospitals are pretty people-intensive 'businesses'; LRI is no exception. It serves around 500,000 patients a year and nearly 75 per cent of its revenue costs are accounted for by direct pay costs. In 1992 LRI was chosen as a pilot site for whole hospital re-engineering and challenged to make 'outrageous improvements'. Less than two years on, the results are impressive; administrative activities reduced by 40 per cent in initial target areas and, by way of example, a neurological outpatients clinic where diagnostic time was typically eight – twelve weeks and three or four visits, now takes a single five-hour visit. The re-engineering programme continues, not spurred by a crisis but from the challenge of achieving further massive improvements in patient care, teaching and research. Staff support has been enthusiastic across all levels and functions as the programme rolls out. A myriad unnecessary processes have been able to be productively either reduced or indeed eliminated; not the least of these processes was the almost universal testing of urine for virtually all conditions! In 1994, the hospital's single visit clinic won the European Golden Helix award for the top healthcare quality initiative in Europe. Its programme is continuing at a hectic pace in making more 'outrageous improvements', to the delight of patients and the considerable satisfaction of staff.

Rank Xerox
A European market leader in document technology, Rank Xerox is a large company with a healthy reputation and a quality oriented culture, linked to measurement thinking. The case relates to the service (maintenance) operation employing some 7,000 people spread over 15 countries. The organisation was not in decline but was in a position of what has been described as 'satisfactory under performance'. Return on assets was generally between 6 and 8 per cent each year. In 1993, the chief executive set out a new vision for growth and reductions in cost but in an 'intelligent manner'. A return on assets target was set at 18 per cent (double the then existing rate), with other key targets relating to Customer Satisfaction, Employee Satisfaction and Market Share. Just over a year into the re-engineering process, return on assets had risen to 13 per cent, with significant progress in all other target areas.

The Royal Bank of Scotland (RBS)
One of the world's oldest banks, having survived 'ups' and 'downs' over nearly 300 years. Since the great depression of the 1930s until the late 1980s, protected by heavy regulation, banks in general, and including RBS, enjoyed unrivalled stability and profitability. Customer groups were, though, severely disadvantaged through lack of competition. Deregulation of the financial services industry, beginning in the late 1980s, led to customers becoming more discriminating. With the opportunities afforded to 'newcomers' in certain sectors of the market, such as building societies and insurance companies, depositors and borrowers started going elsewhere. The scene was, to say the least, less than rosy for RBS. In 1991 a 'revolution' and restructuring started, leading, in 1992, to the start of a dramatic change programme targeted at making the bank 'The best performing financial services institution in the UK by 1997'. Some two years into the programme, the Retail Bank,

now employing 14,000 people, is well on the way and has already turned round its loss-making operations to achieve its target of £200m incremental profit contribution.

Toshiba

Before 1979, Toshiba made no televisions in Europe. In 1979, they gained entry to the protected European market via a joint venture with (and managed by) the Rank Organisation. When, only two years after the commencement, the joint venture ended with Rank withdrawing entirely from the electronic consumer products market, Toshiba was faced with a dilemma: to start again on a greenfield site or to utilise the existing physical and human resources. The latter choice was made with a challenge: in only six months, to provide an entirely new organisational base delivering the highest quality products, consistently and cost-effectively – not something known to the UK television industry.

That meant fundamentally changing operating processes, information systems, and people practices and attitudes. The initiatives preceded the coining of the phrase ' business process re-engineering' but the characteristics of what has been defined as BPR were nevertheless met. The result was an organisation producing at the start, with one-tenth the number of people, about half the former quantity of televisions. Quality standards and consistency were better than anything hitherto deemed possible. The mechanisms which brought about a new era of co-operation were at that time novel. These were introduced instantaneously, with what was known as 'shock treatment'. The foundations have stood the test of time, supporting expansion of television outputs more than five times as large as originally, and admitting expansion into the manufacture of other market-leading products. They have also supported painful shrinkages and market withdrawal in some products. While the original initiatives received much publicity for the novel human resource management practices that were introduced, the case presented here focuses, in a way not hitherto published, on the reasoning behind the change mechanisms and the means for sustaining performance in good times and bad, beyond the 'big step'.

Ingredients and recipes

Is re-engineering another fad? For many organisations, re-engineering will come and go. It's not a strategy for the faint of heart. Yet re-engineering offers an inescapable logic that in our opinion will guarantee its survival. We have built, over decades, organisational structures that just don't fit in with today's need for speed, quality and service, and value. Few can argue the need to overhaul our core processes. In most companies the way we work is painful for us all. Yet, the expectations we have of our employees in a re-engineered environment are unlike any before. We hope *Re-engineering's Missing Ingredient* will provide you with ingredients, if not the recipes, to help you capture the minds and hearts of those that ultimately will make your re-engineering implementation successful – your workforce.

2

GETTING STARTED – AND WHAT SHOULD STOP YOU STARTING

- ☐ Crisis or ambition may trigger re-engineering but both offer uncertain ways forward.
- ☐ Recognising and managing the risks are key to success.
- ☐ Consideration of the human factors from the outset, is essential.
- ☐ Without leadership or active support from top management, success is doubtful.
- ☐ All stakeholders need to be involved.
- ☐ Capability management is at the core of successful re-engineering.
- ☐ Starting without projecting and providing for resources to support HR initiatives will severely undermine success.

Business process re-engineering is a high-risk strategy; that is not in doubt. For those contemplating the kind of sweeping change that characterises BPR, the key issues are recognising the risks and managing the risks.

Assessing risks

Assessing the risks must include the people risks. As shown in the introduction to this book, the vast majority of the step-change initiatives do not succeed in terms of their original intention, significantly through inattention to the people factor. Recognising this and understanding the implications is vital to all the key stakeholders. Understanding may be significantly enhanced through involvement of a human resource specialist, well-versed in the dimensions of:

1   strategic human resource management and its sub-sets, and

2   the processes required to bring about successful change.

Indeed, it might be that the senior HR practitioner triggers the thinking that brings about the major change involved in understanding the opportunities as well as the requirements for fundamental alteration of the people processes within the organisation. One recent study has shown that in more than 30 companies in Scotland, successful fundamental change has not only been led by but was initiated by the principal human resource practitioner in those organisations.[30] That is the view of their respective chief executives.

From the studies undertaken so far into the success or otherwise of business process re-engineering initiatives, the singular lesson must be that consideration of the people factor before starting must be a prerequisite. Otherwise neither the right initiatives to bring about sustainable and harmonious organisational effectiveness nor the financial resources required to bring about effective change are likely to be pin-pointed. Like in the children's board game 'Snakes and Ladders', going back to 'go' is both unsatisfying and unproductive. 'Snakes and Ladders' depends solely upon the chance throw of a dice. In the real world, the odds are significantly in the hands of the planners and starters.

Crisis and opportunity

Business re-engineering initiatives are typically founded on a business imperative or crisis. This can be a crisis of opportunity, or a crisis of failure. The radical kind of change characterised by BPR is rarely initiated because someone merely thinks it would be a good idea to do something different, such as reduce costs. If it does start that way then the change process might be already doomed to failure in that it will be harder to sustain a shared vision. There is nothing like a crisis to focus people's minds but crises are often responded to with short-term solutions.

Not all BPR initiatives are kicked into play by crisis. Xerox in the USA probably learned much out of crisis in the early 1980s when it had fundamentally to rethink its business in the face of Japanese competition, but the initiative illustrated within Rank Xerox in Europe was hardly crisis, just significant under-performance highlighted by the Chief Executive particularly in relation to return on assets. Their attention and an already in-built culture used to assessing and managing by facts, clearly was a sufficient trigger when coupled with clear and resolute top-down leadership. Through benchmarking, the potential for improved performance in Rank Xerox became clear. In the case of The Leicester Royal Infirmary there was unquestionably no 'crisis' that motivated a starting point. Their re-engineering programme was led by a vision triggered originally by a challenge from the NHS Regional General Manager seeking to bring about 'outrageous improvement' for patients in a specific area. The excitement of what was proved to be capable of being done appears to have been the spur to the adoption of a global programme of change across the hospital.

Starting all over again

The speed at which business process re-engineering is delivered should not be confused with short-termism. What has to be delivered needs to be fundamental and provide the solution of 'If we were starting again, how we would we ideally choose to organise ourselves?' Starting again, literally or metaphorically, is a brave strategy and the range of the change will substantially depend upon the trigger that causes the change to be considered.

Exemplar starters

The triggers for sweeping and fundamental change amongst the companies, illustrated as case studies in this book, are many and varied. The Royal Bank of Scotland was ailing; its Branch Banking Division was losing money and losing credibility in a highly competitive business, itself subject to wide-spread change within the financial services industry. Tinkering and applying short-term solutions would do nothing for its future. For a bank established some 300 years ago, the thought of 'no future' for a substantial part of its business brought about an uncompromising response, 'to be, within five years, the best retail bank in Britain'. Coupled with this vision was the assumption that the 'best retail bank' would be not only viable but financially profitable. The trigger for the Royal Bank of Scotland, then, was the need to survive, coupled with an opportunity to build a 'new' and better business.

Rank Xerox was not, on the face of it, in crisis but their competitive position and, in particular, their return on assets employed were way below their vision of 'ideal' and, if they were to stay competitively in business, a much higher return was required. Further, through extensive benchmarking they ascertained that, operationally, their European organisation was way behind in the league of comparable organisations. Initiated and spurred on by the chief executive, the organisation set some new high standards.

In the case of Toshiba, the trigger was an unequivocal need to start again or, at best, substantially lose existing and future market share. In the extreme, they might even have needed to withdraw from supplying, within Europe, what was, world-wide, one of its core strategic products – televisions.

Bass Taverns was the rump-end business of an industry undergoing massive external interference requiring them to 'lose' nearly half of their 7,000 managed public houses that were themselves subject to changing customer habits. Customers were, nationally, spending less on both food and drinks in pubs.

In the case of The Leicester Royal Infirmary National Health Trust, the issue could, at the level of that hospital, be said to be more of a challenge than a crisis. It was part of the system universally under pressure from its 'customers', relative to the level of service provided, as well as from its staff who, in the National Health Service generally, were not known for having a high level of satisfaction with the system within which they were operating, and from the Government, which was, through its hierarchy of agencies, looking for a step-change in efficiency and service (upwards) coupled with a step-change in costs (downwards).

Stakeholder support and sponsorship

What characterises the 'trigger' in each of these cases are the actions of the top manager for the time being in office. In every case, each of the case study organisations had a top manager who both understood and articulated the difficulties and challenges to be faced and who understood and accepted the risks implicit in undertaking the scale of change required. But few people, except in their own business, go forward with massive capital investment without engaging the commitment of others.

Shareholders, parent companies or organisational paymasters have, as a minimum, to give tacit support coupled with acceptance or direct contribution of the financial wherewithal necessary to move forward. None of this is likely to be forthcoming without acknowledgement of the commitment of the overall top management team. So, the people to be 'engaged' into the need for change, with a recognition of the risks for change are:

1   the chief executive of the major business unit involved, and
2   the chief executive of the overall organisation and that top team, and
3   the 'parent' or paymaster.

Where the acceptance of the need for major change starts (say, with the chief executive), is less important than that the people at each of these three levels accept wholeheartedly that need, before moving forward. At least five conditions have to be accepted by this group:

1   The adverse consequences of maintaining the *status quo*.
2   The potential benefit or gain of the projected future state.
3   The impact upon operational processes.
4   The impact upon systems.
5   The impact upon people; their values, attitudes, knowledge, skills and behaviours (individually and collectively).

If the project is to move forward with any chance of sustained commitment, one of the top team needs to assume the role of 'project sponsor'. Where the sponsor is at too low a level, is seen to be partisan or perhaps lacks the personal charisma to carry through the necessary support, chance of success will be substantially undermined. It is the sponsor who needs to be very visible in providing support and advice, particularly of an internal political kind. The chief executive is the obvious choice but other top team champions are also appropriate. More than tacit support from the chief executive is at least required.

Customers and suppliers as stakeholders

Much thought needs to be spared for two other sets of people who are stakeholders: the customers and suppliers. As regards suppliers, Toshiba set out to treat their component and services suppliers as much as part of their internal team as their employees. Their attitudes and behaviours had to change as much as those inside the company. Without a step-change from them, the new 'machine' that had been designed would not be able to function. The distinction between 'inside' and 'outside' employees is increasingly getting less clear. Suppliers more and more include not just those who have a classic selling relationship with the organisation. Temporary, job-share, seasonal, occasional, sub-contract and specialist support people are now much more part of making things happen in the desired ways. Their commitment needs to be engaged and maintained. Top-down macho-style change can be imposed even less on a much freer thinking and operating group.

Customers are people too! New ways of doing things that are 'efficient' will be worth little if they are not engaged in the process and the implementation. Customers have to be educated and sometimes their behaviour changed, so that they can benefit. But they are not captive and, if they don't feel comfortable, they will probably go elsewhere. Not all customers are free to go elsewhere but some such 'customers' have played and are continuing to play a direct and major role in the re-engineering processes at The Leicester Royal Infirmary. Patient care needs to involve the patients! Without their direct involvement and contribution, the hospital admits that their 'solutions' would have been significantly lacking.

Getting it right

Capability management

A notable feature of organisations that have successfully re-engineered their businesses with sweeping changes is expectation that an organisational strategy and the formulation of such a strategy, if that is under review, goes hand in hand with the development of strategic responsiveness. Strategic responsiveness arises out of a synergy between strategic visioning and capability management. Capability management, in the way that the phrase is used here, is: 'The inclination and ability to engage in behaviour which will optimise attainment of an organisation's near and medium-term objectives' (adapted from Ansoff).[31] A fundamental assertion of this book is that capability management is at the core of successful delivery of re-engineered organisations. Considerations need to be always holistic, with a process emphasis, transcending cross-functional considerations.

Realistic expectations of all of the top team and the financial 'sponsors', are undoubtedly necessary. It is no use getting started on a project that is going to take up to two years if the top team or the financial sponsors will be expecting results in six months or a year. Nor that the, perhaps substantial, capital outlays will be self-funding within the project time-scales, though in some cases significant contributions might be possible. Commencing a major re-engineering effort without adequate recourse to financial resources is likely to be an unmitigated disaster. It is often erroneously believed that BPR projects can be self-funding within their term.

Bold application of resources

While it can be more easily recognised that substantial budgeting will be required for new information technology, etc, the investment in the people side of BPR planning, communications and implementation can match or exceed that required for technology. 'Making do' on the people investments is not a strategy likely to lead to success. Nevertheless, there are strategies that can be adopted that can mitigate risk and provide, at the same time, a 'model' of the means to success.

The notable initiative to be adopted to mitigate risk and

provide a model, is the adoption of a 'prototype' project where the risks of both capital commitment and the commitment of high calibre project participants can be contained. Nevertheless, Michael Hammer who originated the word 're-engineering' in the context of work processes asserts that: 'Re-engineering cannot be planned meticulously and established in small and cautious steps. It's an all-or-nothing proposition with uncertain results.'[32] A tension between Hammer's assertion and prudent management clearly exists, but in successful risk assessment and management the need for caution and moving forwards in a measured way will need to be balanced against the urgencies that are called for in the originating need and vision for change. It should not automatically be assumed, given holistic needs, that a narrow project or one with insufficient depth will be able to offer anything very valuable towards the whole; the impact needs to be on overall performance. This, of its nature, requires projects to have sufficient process breadth.

Prototyping

Essentially, the initial project can be seen as a prototype from which the organisation can learn (with the probability of mistakes being made) rather than a stage of the overall project. The single-visit clinic 'Sigma' project as piloted by The Leicester Royal Infirmary is, nevertheless, an outstandingly good case of a pilot project that provided foundations for a much larger scheme. But prototypes can't successfully be expected to be undertaken by skimping on resources. They are not a 'cheap' way forward. Successful delivery of limited, as well as large projects, requires commitment of the best resources available. The people involved are unlikely to work effectively without adequate facilities and tools, including, where appropriate, specialist management help.

Singularity of purpose

Singularity of purpose is a notable feature of successful BPR projects. Where re-engineering is being undertaken as one of a number of other major initiatives, there are indications that sometimes the focus can become divided as the project competes unsuccessfully or confusingly with other initiatives.

However, both Bass Taverns and Rank Xerox, in a controlled and measured way, admitted wider and related projects at the same time as their BPR initiatives.

The essential elements

At the start point, the human resource implications of getting the people at the top conditioned and supportive, and recognising the impacts on people elsewhere within the organisation, plus the related significant costs of supporting people-related change, are vital. Those starting need a 'Columbus mentality' – not just the mentality of Christopher Columbus himself, but also the mentality of the worthies who had both the vision to believe that the investment they were making in Columbus would be worthwhile plus the capacity to fund that investment, and then let Columbus get on with it. That might be the role for today's sponsors but the senior executives involved will unquestionably have an ongoing role in either a hands-on or hands-off way, in leading their organisation through the period of radical change. The demands of leadership will include a tenacious pursuit of performance objectives and of actions that will enable the engagement of all necessary resources required at the start and throughout the change process. Sustained support, leadership and involvement from the top are ingredients that can substantially affect success. Without them, research suggests that success with BPR is much less likely. Most go further – without top support, don't start.

Bass Taverns – getting started

Bass Taverns embraced the philosophy underpinning BPR in terms of 'starting anew' when it was faced with a business crisis that resulted from the imposition of Department of Trade and Industry orders which forced the sale of some 40 per cent of the company's pubs in less than two years. This huge legislative impact and threat to the business was accompanied by a significant downturn in demand for eating and drinking in pubs, as the recession of the early 1990s really did bite into consumer confidence and expenditure. Morale in the pubs retailing industry was not, to say the least, buoyant. Bright and able staff, among others, were looking to their futures with trepidation, seeking transfers or pastures new. No one really wanted to join the division; potentially it was being seen as a real-time Cinderella. Competitively, the business was faring badly. The task was clear; the company had to sell around 3,000 outlets, regain its competitive position in the market-place and sustain healthy profit and cash-flow contribution to the parent company, Bass Plc. Clearly, something radical had to be done and a fundamental redesign of the way the business was to be run was initiated.

The first initiative was the appointment of the new chief executive with virtually a free hand and the financial where-withal to apply the resources that were necessary. The choice was not, to some observers, obvious. Jimmy Angles was in his late 50s and had been running the Britvic fruit-juice business owned by Bass. Being only some years from retirement his strategy might have been to do the minimum, keep his head down and coast to retirement without in any way being held accountable for what would have happened. But that was not the strategy he adopted. He determined that a solution to the seemingly insurmountable problems could be found and he set about trying to find it. His resolve was unerring and he gained the support of his board.

Bass Taverns, as a company and a newly defined business, was born out of enforced change and adversity. The new chief executive quickly and continuously projected a vision of a radi-cally different organisation to satisfy the demands of a rapidly changing business environment, a vision of:

□   responsiveness and customer focus
□   delivering a whole new range of consumer offerings, to address the segments of the market-place in which the company was weak.

His commitment was never in doubt; he lived and breathed BPR and change programmes, but his involvement was not constantly 'hands on'. Outsiders sometimes ask 'What would you do if you did not have this total commitment from the chief executive officer?' Implicitly and explicitly the answer has remained consistent for the four or more years – 'Don't start!' Without the constant involvement and commitment of the chief executive there is no doubt that the project could not have succeeded.

A potential benefit at the start was work done towards laying the foundations for new computer-based information systems, the investment in which had been massive. What was not known at that time was whether it would deliver sustainable competitive advantage in a business as yet not having finalised its scope and scale. At the heart of this IT infrastructure was the Bass Retail System in the pubs – an effective and incredibly efficient EPOS (electronic point of sale) system, a new property management, financial reporting and purchasing system called 'Project Landmark' and a personnel information and payroll system called 'Project Unity'. These were delivered on a technology platform of every manager having a networked PC and every pub having a back office PC.

Shrinking size threw up some benefits. The shrinkage in the business through sell-off of pubs was already having an effect. Fewer pubs meant less office space required to accommodate fewer support staff, so surplus office accommodation was available in reasonably good measure. A redundant office block was set aside to provide dedicated facilities for the project team who would be taking things forward.

To go forward, commitments and resources were needed which would underpin the capability of success. Those made available from the start, were:

☐ substantial financial resources
☐ 12 of the company's 'brightest and best' functional and line managers, full time, on the project for four months
☐ specialist consultancy support to help define the scope and parameters
☐ dedicated office accommodation away from existing activities
☐ IT and project management resources and support
☐ everyone on the project team being personally 'sponsored' by a member of the company board

The Leicester Royal Infirmary – getting started

The Leicester Royal Infirmary NHS Trust is a large, complex teaching hospital. Each year, around 500,000 patients visit the hospital. It also has a key role in teaching and training nurses, doctors and other healthcare professionals. The third aspect of its key activity is in the capture and application of clinical research. Nearly 75 per cent of the hospital's revenue costs are taken up by direct pay costs, making it a very people intensive business.

The Leicester Royal Infirmary was chosen as one of two National Health Service pilot sites for whole hospital re-engineering. Alongside King's Healthcare NHS Trust, it is the first hospital in Britain and one of the first in the world to undertake such a radical change programme. The circumstance which led The Leicester Royal Infirmary to a re-engineering strategy was its goal to become the best teaching hospital in the country. Given the increasingly complex and turbulent environment in which it operated, incremental approaches were no longer enough. The success of early process redesign activities from 1992 onwards convinced the clinical and managerial leadership of the hospital that a major 'step-change' approach could succeed.

With regard to the imperative for re-engineering, there are many factors in the Trust's wider environment which led it to the conclusion that ongoing incremental improvement was no longer enough.

As the age profile of the population increases, the demand for services gets greater at a time of increasing financial constraint. The creation of the healthcare market and the growth in general practitioner fundholding means that hospitals such as The Leicester Royal Infirmary must secure sufficient contracts from healthcare purchasers to remain viable. Its financial future is dependent on high levels of patient, purchaser and general medical practitioner satisfaction.

Within healthcare generally there is a move away from large city centre acute hospitals towards community-based health services in local areas. In the era of the Patient's Charter, patient expectations are growing enormously. Finally, an explosion is taking place in medical advances: conventional X-ray technology is being replaced by digital imaging; experiments in bloodless surgery may fundamentally challenge the basis of conventional surgery.

In the context of the drive for re-engineering, these factors might point to a crisis-motivated starting point. In fact, the opposite is the case. The Leicester Royal Infirmary re-engineering programme is led by ambition. This is characterised by its mission statement from the hospital's *Strategic Direction*: 'We at The Leicester Royal Infirmary NHS Trust will work together to become the best hospital in the country, with an outstanding local and national reputation for our treatment, research and teaching. We will give to each patient the same care and consideration we would to our own family.'

All these strategic factors led to the conclusion that the Trust could not carry on with the type of incremental change that was taking place. Each year, the hospital cut a few percentage points off of its operating budget, continually chipping away at the heart of its clinical services. Achievement of the *Strategic Direction* would require quality targets far beyond those set down in the Patient's Charter. The starting point for The Leicester Royal Infirmary's re-engineering journey was September 1992 with the establishment of the Sigma project. This was set up by the NHS Regional General Manager who wanted to bring about 'outrageous improvement' in healthcare services. His support enabled The Leicester Royal Infirmary to set up a series of projects in outpatient clinics.

The most successful of these was the neurology single-visit clinic. Previously, patients with a range of neurological symptoms would typically wait between eight and twelve weeks for diagnosis. The process involved an initial consultation with a consultant, return visits to the hospital for a range of complex investigations, followed by a further visit to the consultant for diagnosis and treatment plan (see Figure 2.1). This required the patient to make three or four hospital visits. This process was redesigned into one, five-hour visit (see Figure 2.2). The patient saw the consultant at the beginning of the clinic, all the investigations were prescheduled and the results were available for a final consultation at the end of the clinic. The outcomes exceeded expectations. The levels of patient and GP satisfaction have remained very high. It has been possible to reduce the level of administrative activity by 40 per cent as the process has been streamlined. The single-visit clinic won the Hewlett Packard Golden Helix Award for the top healthcare quality initiative in Europe.

Figure 2.1

THE LEICESTER ROYAL INFIRMARY NEUROLOGY CLINIC BEFORE RE-ENGINEERING

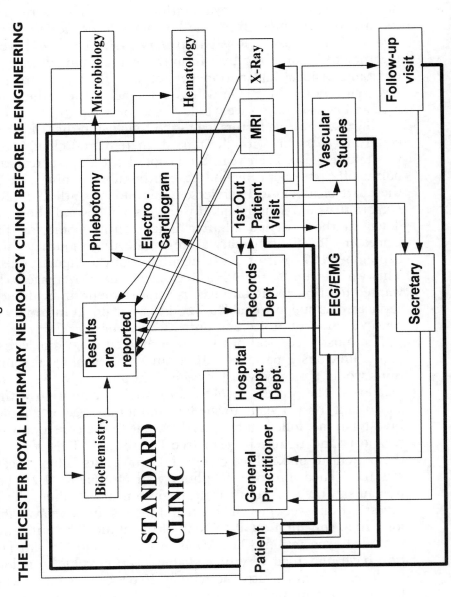

Figure 2.2

THE LEICESTER ROYAL INFIRMARY NEUROLOGY CLINIC AFTER RE-ENGINEERING AS A 'SINGLE-VISIT' CLINIC

Re-designed Clinic

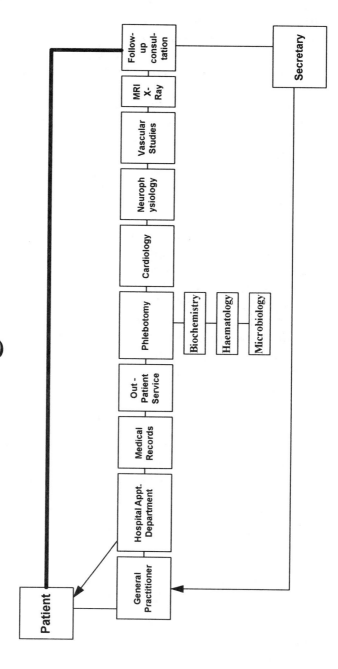

This was not, however, enough. Although The Leicester Royal Infirmary was able to develop a number of single-visit clinics, offering superb patient service, it wanted to deliver the same level of 'outrageous improvement' across the hospital. The key learning from the Sigma project was that a very radical approach was required to transform the hospital's operational processes. It needed to reinvent the way it delivered healthcare from a patient's perspective.

Measured against a range of national criteria, The Leicester Royal Infirmary was considered to be an efficient NHS provider. However, process analysis, carried out across the hospital, identified significant inefficiency, 'non-value adding' activity, and potential for delay, duplication and error. An incremental approach was not enough. Nothing less than 'zero-based' redesign of the entire hospital system was required. As preparation for the whole hospital re-engineering effort, a significant programme of planning and research was embarked upon. This involved linking up with re-engineering programmes and re-engineering experts on a global basis. The Trust's chief executive equates the effort that was invested in planning the re-engineering programme to that of setting up and planning the building of a new hospital.

Dramatic results have been achieved at the early stages of the programme:

- [ ] With regard to the Patient's Charter standard for outpatients seen within 30 minutes of appointment time, The Leicester Royal Infirmary has jumped from the bottom of the league table to near to the top. Over a 12-month period, 51 years of patient waiting time has been saved.
- [ ] The level of patient service previously offered to a few hundred people at the single-visit clinics is now routinely available to many thousands of patients attending re-engineered clinics.
- [ ] Previously it took an average of 79 hours for the results of a range of routine diagnostic tests to be available. Now the results are guaranteed within one hour.

Many of the principles learned during this invaluable research phase have remained cornerstones of the Trust's re-engineering approach.

1   The critical role of leadership

☐ Managing in the public sector creates many unique problems. External (governmental) constraints can limit flexibility and autonomy. Broad accountability is required and performance expectations may continually shift. There are many limitations to leadership autonomy. In this context, the importance of senior management leadership of the re-engineering programme cannot be underestimated. The chief executive of The Leicester Royal Infirmary devotes at least 30 per cent of his time to the programme. The management of the external environment is a key aspect of his re-engineering role.

☐ Equally important is the role of clinical leadership. Hospitals have specific characteristics which create particular challenges for organisational transformation.

☐ Hospitals may employ up to 40 different disciplines or professions, each the product of professionally focused education and training.

☐ Many hospital staff may have professional and individual career goals which are not necessarily aligned with the corporate vision.

☐ Given the professional model, the hospital hierarchy does not accurately reflect the actual power system. Culture is harder to change unless it is done through the professional group.

☐ Re-engineering fundamentally challenges the boundaries of much professional organisation. It requires shifts in thinking and practice at the level of individual clinician.

☐ The aim of the re-engineering programme at The Leicester Royal Infirmary is to transform patient care, teaching and research processes. This concentrates on the clinical and professional heartlands of the hospital's activity. The programme is characterised by active leadership by senior clinicians. This is a critical success factor.

2   Quality focus

 □ The focus of the programme is on achieving the *Strategic Direction* through improvements in healthcare delivery, teaching and research. It is not a cost-cutting exercise. Any savings made as a result of the re-engineering programme are reinvested in clinical services, in line with clinical priorities.

 □ The experience of re-engineering at The Leicester Royal Infirmary suggests that it would have been very difficult to engage clinical colleagues in a cost-driven programme and the results would be less dramatic.

3   Up-front investment of resources

 □ Typically within the NHS, change programmes are led by one or two individuals working full time on the project, with many more participating on top of their normal jobs.

 □ Within The Leicester Royal Infirmary, up to 30 members of staff have been seconded full time at critical design phases of the programme, with many hundreds more playing active roles in the process. Such dedicated resource has enabled the re-engineering programme to move forward at a much faster pace than experienced previously. The level and pace of change required could not have been achieved without this commitment.

4   Organisation-wide focus on key processes

 □ Rather than concentrating on single departments or clinical specialities, the redesign teams have re-engineered core healthcare delivery, teaching and research processes which cut across the whole organisation. Generic processes are designed which are adapted to the needs of specific patient groups (see Figure 2.3).

 The organisation-wide approach has brought many advantages. It has:

 (a) led to better solutions, optimising the potential within the system

 (b) led to more rapid and effective benefits realisation

(c) helped to balance the management of a partially re-engineered organisation with running 'business as usual'.

5   Involvement of key internal and external stakeholders

☐ Much of the re-engineering literature suggests a linear/rational model of change characterised by extensive baseline analysis and process mapping, combined with meticulous project planning. The profile of the change experienced at The Leicester Royal Infirmary is complex and multidimensional and often unpredictable. The social, political and cultural aspects are often the determinants as to whether the programme will move ahead. Therefore, an extensive programme of communication and involvement with key internal and external stakeholders has been an important programme component.

Figure 2.3

THE LEICESTER ROYAL INFIRMARY HEALTHCARE PROCESS MAP

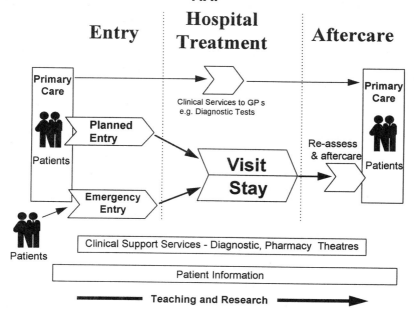

The Leicester Royal Infirmary continues to achieve dramatic results as its programme unfolds. The challenge is set by Michael Hammer in a letter to the Trust's chief executive: 'There may be no contemporary initiative more important nor more complex than the re-engineering of health care delivery processes. Not only does such an effort offer the prospect of dramatic cost savings and improvements in the quality of medical care, it can also service as a template for re-engineering across the entire public sector.'

Rank Xerox – getting started

Rank Xerox was originally founded on the opportunity of explosive growth in a new market created by the Xerox copier product, and on patent protection. Growth in the 1960s and 1970s was limited only by ability to develop marketing and manufacturing capacity to meet customer demand. The organisation grew organically, with limited controls and a culture of success. Such pride usually has an end, and for Rank Xerox the end of the initial growth phase arrived in the late 1970s. Japanese competition captured the mass-market sector with high-quality and low-cost products, then began to erode the heartland of the Rank Xerox business. Rank Xerox market share fell rapidly, and a period of cost cutting and soul searching ensued.

Xerox in the USA experienced the same pattern of decline and their chief executive, David Kearns, set in motion the response, based on Fuji Xerox's early experience in total quality management, that saved the company. Benchmarking, now a frequently used tool, was developed by Xerox in the early 1980s. The research proved that Xerox had to compete with Japanese products that were selling at less than Xerox manufacturing cost. Kearns directed a world-wide programme of total quality, aimed at:

☐ improving product quality and reducing manufacturing costs

☐ focusing on customer satisfaction

☐ changing behaviour patterns to concentrate on continuous improvement, by internal co-operation and teamwork.

The programme, known as 'Leadership Through Quality', was

developed by a team of executives from across the world; Xerox was not prepared to accept the standard consultant solution and created a corporate quality culture which was cascaded throughout the Xerox world. This can still be observed in meetings, posters and team events to this day. The 'Quality Policy' still holds:

> Rank Xerox is a Quality Company.
> Quality is the basic business principle for Rank Xerox.
> Quality means providing our external and internal customers with innovative products and services that fully satisfy their requirements.
> Quality improvement is the job of every employee.

Rank Xerox made good progress in the 1980s, developing continuous growth in profit and revenue. Many improvements were implemented, in manufacturing quality and cost, in product development, in asset management, and particularly in the management of customer satisfaction, through regular customer surveys, closed-loop response systems and rewarding employees on results. Customer satisfaction approached 100 per cent in some countries. Employee satisfaction developed as a priority, with annual surveys and quality improvement teams to take action on problem areas. In 1992 Rank Xerox won the European Quality Award in the first year of presentation. However, the clear successes of Leadership Through Quality were not yet translated into the required level of ambitious growth.

Rank Xerox prides itself on 'managing by fact'. It rigorously measures progress on corporate priorities for all products, geographic areas and functions. The organisation defines its corporate priorities as:

> Customer satisfaction
> Employee satisfaction
> Market share
> Return on assets

The model defines that achievement of the first two priorities will lead to the third and fourth. The key priority is Return on Assets, where the corporate target was consistently set at 18 per cent. Rank Xerox, equally consistently, was operating at

6–7 per cent, or 8 per cent in a really good year – what might be called 'satisfactory under performance'.

Despite all the rewards and successes brought by quality, including survival itself, bottom-line results were still sluggish. It is difficult to observe when this was translated into a crisis, this time one of opportunity, but managing director Bernard Fournier concluded that enough was enough in late 1992 – the very year of the European Federation of Quality Management (EFQM) prize. Having decided that the opportunity existed, he wasted no time in making it public, and employees learned of his intentions in a *Financial Times* article. He made clear that he wanted growth, major reductions in cost (over $200m per year) and he wanted to achieve this in an intelligent manner – through process re-engineering. The EFQM assessment had concluded that while Rank Xerox made good progress on process management, building on quality experience, there was still major opportunity in simplification of organisation and working practices. Fournier, a very pragmatic Frenchman, was determined to break through the static return on assets barrier, and certainly faced a potential personal crisis if he failed to deliver.

Royal Bank of Scotland – getting started

Since the great depression of the 1930s until the late 1980s, the financial services sector generally, and banks in particular, had enjoyed unrivalled stability and profitability. The banking industry was heavily regulated and costs of entry to their markets high. To a large extent, regulation stifled competition and as a consequence the banks had little need to pay attention to their customers. Two customer groups were particularly disadvantaged – the individual depositors, who were never able to realise the full value of their assets because of interest rate restrictions, and the larger borrowers, who invariably were major businesses who paid more for their loans than the risk would justify.

The combination of 'Big Bang' in 1986, the stock market crash of October 1987 and the UK Financial Services Act effectively deregulated the British financial services industry, which has since proved to be a watershed for banking in the UK. As a consequence, the larger borrowers began to seek alternative sources of funding. In addition, the individual depositors were attracted to a wider range of higher interest products, offered by building societies, insurers and even central government through its various bond issues. Increased competition, together with the high levels of lending in the property market, which went into terminal decline throughout the UK from the late 1980s to the mid-1990s, resulted in the banks amassing frightening levels of bad debts. This was further exacerbated by the debt of third-world countries, with little chance of repayment.

The combination of bad debts, lack of underlying profit and costs of 63 per cent of income in 1991 provided the Royal Bank of Scotland with the imperative to take action. An analysis of the Royal Bank's core businesses by the newly appointed chief executive, Dr George Mathewson, led him to believe that the bank could become 'The best performing Financial Services Institution in the UK by 1997' if dramatic action was taken. What had paralysed his predecessors was balancing the risk factors associated with change, which included the need for high levels of investment, against the need to generate income and reduce costs.

Mathewson recognised the need both to treat the paralysis and break up the powerful regional all-purpose bank and, in doing so, create a divisionalised bank focused on distinct customer segments and led by people who shared his beliefs and vision. The most dramatic signal of change had been Mathewson's appointment. It was followed by a secret planning exercise which was known as 'Nova Reda'. It later became synonymous with a day in 1991 when the 'old guard' on the executive were swept away. Shortly after, the bank was split into three, a Wholesale Bank, a Retail Bank and an Operations Division, created to provide, among other things, the core essential services of property, information technology, human resources and purchasing.

In addition to the casualties of 'Nova Reda', a further assessment of the executive or leadership group of 60 convinced Mathewson that carrying out the quantum and dramatic re-engineering necessary to achieve his vision would require wholesale changes in this group. Between 1992 and 1995, the size and characteristics of the executive population changed significantly. Over 30 new executives were recruited from other organisations, a significant proportion of whom had never worked in banking. The educational profile of the leadership group also changed – in the past it was a 'normal' career path to join the bank on leaving school at 16 or 18 and, for the lucky or the diligent, to aspire to a main board position after 35 years. Few in the old leadership group had university degrees, nor had many worked in other organisations or industries. In Mathewson's view, few were equipped to lead substantial and sustained change to achieve the new vision

Figure 2.4

MIND-SET RE-ENGINEERING, ROYAL BANK OF SCOTLAND

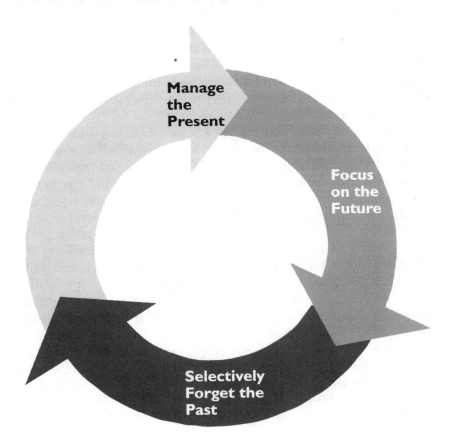

It was, however, not enough just to change the faces at the top; the underlying ills of the industry generally, and the Royal Bank in particular, required fundamental review, where tough basic questions had to be asked and answers sought. They could no longer rely on the tacit assumptions that had seen the bank survive the previous 280 years. What was required was for the bank to go back to basics and take a zero-based approach to every process throughout the organisation, which, in the context of the bank, was akin to changing the engines on a jumbo jet in mid-air. It was necessary to get all managers to review their model of the world, to make the transition from being convergent thinkers in a command and control bureaucracy to being given permission to think divergently and question everything. In reality, what was required could be termed 'mind-set re-engineering', where the bank needed its managers to focus on the future, manage the present and selectively forget some of their 280 years of history (Figure 2.4).

While the whole bank has undergone dramatic change, this case discusses the 'change programme' carried out in the retail bank. This division employs 14,000 staff supporting the branch network, and in April 1992 a five-year change programme was launched with the title 'Columbus'. The Columbus Change Programme was charged with responsibility to re-engineer the business processes and provide the shape for the bank of the future, and in doing so, achieve an improvement in profitability of £200m.

Toshiba – getting started

It was a 'life or death' business imperative that brought about fundamental change for Toshiba in Plymouth. The imperative was the ending of a joint venture. Toshiba televisions had hitherto been made by a company owned jointly by Toshiba and the Rank Organisation, established in 1978. It was announced, barely two years from that date, that the joint venture was to come to an end. The joint operation, while lacking ideal requisites of both partners, could by no means be viewed as a failure. It was however fundamentally affected by a strategic decision by Rank to withdraw entirely from the consumer electronics market.

The ultimate outcome was that the same Toshiba products (televisions) were to be manufactured by Toshiba alone, using the same people at the same place but virtually everything else (manufacturing processes, systems and control processes and human resource management processes) was to be entirely new. The critical element was lack of time, which was constrained in absolute terms. From the date of the announcement to having to go it alone, Toshiba had only about six months to make alternative arrangements.

Choices open to Toshiba included broadly maintaining the *status quo* with what were considered to be less than ideal foundations, or doing something entirely different and hopefully laying a new base on which a more efficient, flexible and durable organisation might be built. Decisions had to be made; there were no alternative supplies of televisions available to Toshiba in Europe. Owing to voluntary restrictions on the importation of televisions from Japan, it was not possible for Toshiba to obtain supplies from there. The only other sources of televisions within Europe were from direct competitors and that was unthinkable as well as impracticable. The options were for Toshiba to (a) withdraw and virtually give up their toehold share of the European market for televisions, (b) set up an entirely new manufacturing facility in Europe on a green-field site and allow competitors to take their share in the meantime, or (c) maintain some continuity using resources from the joint venture located at Plymouth. To avoid serious damage to business there was little choice; Toshiba had, if at all possible, to stay at Plymouth. To decide to start again with a completely new organisational framework was unquestionably more difficult.

The easier decision would have been to accept the *status quo* and bring about any required changes on an incremental basis. Early operational considerations, particularly the human resource related issues, drew a key group of UK-based senior management to the conclusion, however, that concentrated 'pain' balanced by potential 'joy' in participating in something entirely new was preferable to a succession of hard-fought remedial measures over time. There would be little chance in those circumstances for things to be under control and, in a rapidly changing and fiercely competitive market, control coupled with flexibility was seen to be vital. This pointed to the need for something new, in which everyone could share; to create a new culture and way of working. Going into uncharted territory would be very risky but the alternatives seemed to have considerable scope for disaggregation and little certainty for real contribution.

The scene was notionally set for something entirely new but neither those who were to have accountability for things on the ground in the UK, nor the ultimate parent company back in Japan, could at that stage have foreseen the extent and novelty of many of the changes that were to be forthcoming. Had these been initially mooted, it is more than possible that Japan would have considered the risks too great. In the event, sea-change initiatives, particularly human resource policy matters, emerged. All that was started with was a need for an efficient manufacturing company working to highest quality standards with a vision of it being operated, from the top down, by locals.

The 'father' of the localisation concept was Mr Kenichiro Hiyama, chairman of Toshiba (U.K.) Ltd, the new manufacturing unit's holding company. His vision was for an essentially British company under British management; different in kind, then, from any other Japanese inward investor. The technical visionary of what needed to be achieved in quality terms was Mr 'Kaz' Komada. Not only was Mr Komada highly competent technically (earlier chief engineer of Toshiba's Fukaya television factory, the largest factory of its kind in the world) he had, for two years, been the senior technical representative of Toshiba in the joint venture company. His sharp-eyed observations and gentle questioning of employees over two years in the UK had equipped him with a keen sense of what was possible with the people and processes he had been working with. Mike Oram, Toshiba UK's Director of Personnel and Company Secretary, had been engaged by Mr Hiyama three years beforehand to 'lay the personnel management foundations for future profitable growth of Toshiba'.

What Toshiba needed, to really 'deliver' a new organisation in the amazingly tight time-scale available, was an overall project manager; if possible, a manufacturing manager of proven capability. It was Toshiba's amazing good fortune to be able to secure the services, on secondment from Rank, of Geoffrey

Deith. Only months beforehand Deith had been appointed managing director of the joint venture company and he had greatly impressed Toshiba colleagues. He was, upon Toshiba's request as part of the break-up arrangements, to be made available to Toshiba for a limited period. Deith had been one of Rank's lead negotiators in the disengagement of the parties from the joint venture, but immediately after settlement being reached he had to assume new loyalties and focus which he did with creative enthusiasm and flair. Mike Oram recalls that, immediately following the conclusion of negotiations, Deith and he compared notes of their respective visions for the new enterprise and found considerable concurrence. There were, at least, to be no political divisions. From that moment, there was a sense of a single team with a single purpose: how to form the most efficient television manufacturing company that was, in the circumstances, possible. The next stage was to select the wider project team and agree the standards and processes that would secure operational viability.

3

BRINGING THE TEAM TOGETHER – VITAL SELECTION

- Allocating the best people, full time, is a key starting point.
- For team selection, attitude of members is at least as important as ability.
- Representation by personnel and development specialists is critical.
- Leaders of re-engineering projects need special qualities.
- Process support and coaching by external resources are features of most successful projects.
- The personal qualities of individual consultants are at least as important as the methodologies and reputation of their firms.

No one doubts that the most important resources for an organisation are its people. If one group of people is going to have a significant impact upon the destiny of the organisation then the identification selection of those people will be the singular act from which all else in a business processing re-engineering initiative will flow.

Selection for what?

All rational selection will start with a question 'What are we selecting *for*?' The incautious or, in a company sense, politically inclined, may well not consider that 'selection' of the top team is an issue and not make any rational assessment of the qualities needed and the balance of those qualities among the team in order to bring about the vision that they might have in mind. Whether or not a conscious analysis of the factors is entered into, the success of the process will be significantly affected by the make-up of the succession of teams that are called into play to design, develop and implement.

The team which is brought together to assess the opportunities and conceptualise the way forward will be the foundation for all that follows; with the speed at which things roll forward there will be little chance for a second go. The team that sets out, needs, through its learning and bonding processes, to be the team that arrives with the answers. Like any amalgam designed for a purpose, the ingredients are vital.

Span of representation
Understanding that the major organisational change characterised by BPR will span the key areas of operational processes, people and technology, it follows that expertise and knowledge spanning all of these will be required. If the IT and HR people are not involved in the early stages of visioning as well as the subsequent stages of business process redesign and implementation, important issues may well be overlooked. Anecdotal comment and some research supports the assertion that in many organisations, the information systems function and the human resource management function are not held in high esteem. That may be an issue either of the quality of the people within the organisation or the lack of recognition of qualities yet to be identified. When line managers initiate re-engineering projects and leave IT and HR specialists out, plans will almost certainly not take into account sufficiently the people and technology dimensions that can lead to effective step-change. Lack of representation at the earlier stages may be compounded in latter stages by functional representatives not working wholeheartedly for project success because they perceive original and maybe fundamental design gaps. Notably, all of the organisations featured as case studies in this book have significant individuals who have represented all key functional inputs. If capability management is what is required, the

inclination and ability to engage in behaviour which will optimise attainment of an organisation's near and medium-term
objectives, then the capability of those involved, expressed in
such terms, sets the standard required.

Immediate versus longer-term requirements

Inclination is a starting point. Optimism and lack of fear may
be subsets of inclination that allow things to be taken forward.
If the issues to be addressed arise out of crisis, crisis itself may
create fear and even panic. Fear drives out optimism. Optimism is essential for creatively generating ways forward. Team
members at any level therefore must feel sufficiently secure in
their own abilities and standing to 'survive'. Managing reassignment and exit processes is dealt with later but must be
taken into account at the stage of selection, particularly in
respect of internal candidates. Individuals who feel in any way
personally under threat will not give of their best. Security need
not, however, be defined in terms of a long-term contract. Security to perform the task, to make a contribution and to go on
to something else can be sufficient, if made explicitly. Indeed,
the very qualities that one might look for in terms of long-term
stability and the capability to manage on an ongoing basis
might not be the qualities that one is looking for in the make-
up of a BPR project team's membership. Here are some of the
desirable qualities.

Attitude

The actual ability of each team member, coupled with attitude,
are the qualities that make for capability. While the case study
organisations in this book are quite different from each other,
there is a similarity in terms of the nature of abilities required
of their project team members. All of the organisations have
emphasised the importance of knowledge and ability, and of
necessary 'functional representation' that bring appropriate
skills and knowledge of information technology and ways and
means of managing the people issues. These are all 'givens' for a
successful outcome. What is a particular feature arising from
the combined experience of the case studies in this book is the
level of agreement that they have, as regards the personal qualities required.

Project leaders need special qualities

For the project leader or team leader, the leadership qualities were shown; a self-evident visionary thinking capability, coupled sometimes with charisma, are notable. Uniformly, high level communication capability is a feature. The capability to think divergently 'well outside the box' is also notable and, if a functional specialist, does not sit narrowly within his or her function. Ideally, the team leader should have wide cross-functional experience. There is a need for resolution to pursue something as difficult, maybe, as finding the Holy Grail … and the energy to maintain that pursuit. Leading in a participative way rather than directing seems to be valuable. These are therefore coupled with physical and mental stamina to stay the course. While most of the project leaders in the case study organisations are male, all the case study contributors conceded that project leaders having 'female' sensitivities (as generally described by Hofstede[33]) rather than 'macho male' sensitivities, bring the widest value. Pre-eminent among these is the ability to listen. Active listening in the project environment is as important as the capability to provide creative input. Other notable qualities which have been appreciated are the ability to manage political issues and defend outrageous ideas. A sense of humour is always appreciated.

General attributes

In terms of the wider team, similar capabilities in terms of creativity, resilience and diversity in thinking have been the issues commonly commented upon. Knowledge of functional specialisms on the basis that these are represented in a balanced way within the team are required and this seems more valued where the individuals' capabilities are acknowledged and respected widely within the organisation. Being the strong functional advocate is quite different from the politically motivated functionary defending or promoting narrow functional issues. Good self-management capability is required in order to reliably support and link with other team members.

Availability

All of the aforementioned personal qualities and abilities will be of insufficient value unless fully made available. Toshiba was the only case where, in the planning stages the team members were not made available on a full-time basis, and this was for very particular operational reasons in that company. It was compensated in part by the excessive hours put in by all of the team members during a very concentrated period. In every other case all the organisations emphasise that they would not have been able to achieve what they have without full-time commitment of the individuals concerned. All of them indicate that it is necessary to make available the most capable individuals within the organisation and this has been, within the case study companies, always at the sacrifice of otherwise important operational requirements. It is suggested that allocating what might widely be perceived as the very best people to the project will itself give a message to others that the organisation really means business.

Using consultants

At The Leicester Royal Infirmary, the involvement of leading medical consultants working in partnership with managers from the chief executive downwards undoubtedly sent a message of a very positive kind. The mechanisms for determining project leaders and team members in all the successful cases illustrated in this book lacks the application of overt scientific method. None of them lacked application of rigour. Some had significant vision. Given the risk, all the organisations involved appeared to have given considerable thought and attention to selection, relative to the range of qualities outlined. Proof of the causal relationship between the quality of selection and quality of achievement, while yet to be made, is not something that most would demand. Sloppiness in selection will nevertheless inevitably lead to sloppiness in output.

External consultants were not used in either the Rank Xerox or the Toshiba cases for quite different reasons. In Rank Xerox's case that organisation has developed process analysis and process capability delivery mechanisms over a number of years and had substantial internal capability to deliver. In Toshiba's case, the time-scale required for action was so short that it was considered that by the time consultants had been briefed and assuming immediate availability, the project would have already been half-way through. In all other cases there is universal acknowledgement of the value added by external consultants. Their value and input can be summarised as:

1   providing a kick-start in terms of conceptual thinking and thinking beyond the experience of the organisational and the internal team members
2   providing technical and analytical tools to help identify options, tools to manage the project and tools to manage the process
3   coaching in new management models and methods
4   adding 'expert' capability and knowledge in specialist areas such as information systems.

Knowing when to bring consultants in is easier than knowing how to recognise when they are no longer needed, but that also needs to be planned and implemented.

Those organisations using consultants observe that it is the value of individual consultants that matters more than the methodologies that the firm itself might bring. The Leicester Royal Infirmary contracted for individual named consultants.

In considering whether or not consultants are needed, the positive reasons are:

☐   if you will benefit from process consultancy skills to get you kick-started
☐   if you need expert knowledge, for example information system trends and opportunities
☐   if you need expert project management methodology
☐   if you wish to draw more widely from other BPR experience
☐   if you need an extra external influence on top management.

If you can satisfy all of these internally you probably don't need external consultants but, even if you don't use external resources directly, an external viewpoint can always be useful. In Toshiba's case, although they did not use consultants, they tested ideas out with external experts.

External support from consultants is much more likely to be needed at the front end, but delivery of implementation demands particular skills and expertise which external experts can also bring. Support in communications, provisions of new skills and comprehension of new systems are all inputs that can be valuable.

External support to bring about changes, particularly in managerial and supervision roles and the need for new skills in those areas such as coaching and instructional skills, and co-operative conflict resolution, have all proved to be valuable.

A lesson from all the players in this book is to undertake careful consideration and selection of external consultants, based upon the qualities needed in the particular organisation rather than the supposed reputation of consultancy providers. External resources will, for the time they are utilised, be as much part of the internal team as those within the organisation. Personal chemistry and the personal qualities sought for internal participants need to be emulated and in some cases exceeded by external consultants.

External specialist help can be extraordinarily expensive. It should never be assumed that because the most expensive or apparently well-known consultants are being used success will be assured. There are notable failures that have cost the employing companies millions and even company collapse. Of the 70 per cent or so of companies that have 'failed', a proportion of these have almost certainly used extensive external resources. Care in the selection of external resources is as important as in the selection of internal resources.

Bass Taverns – bringing the team together

The very best available people in both core business activity and management skills were brought together. In addition to the main project team of 12 people there were 73 full-time staff working on sub-projects, mostly with operations backgrounds. The reasoning was simple – if we were going to transform the way we ran the business then it had to start in the pubs and then work its way through to support staff in offices.

The project leader was the director of corporate change. He defined his job title and, before he took the job on, insisted that at every board meeting, change would be the first item on the agenda, and that he would have at least the first hour of every such meeting to introduce or report on the change programme, as the BPR initiative came to be called. He was and is an outstanding presenter and communicator and this access and these skills were essential prerequisites to the successful implementation of major change and the crucial area of top management commitment. He had previously been the managing director of the Bass Lease Company where he had been responsible for the 1,400 leased pubs that Bass rents to independent lessees. His background was, therefore, sales and general management. He was credible and convincing as well as a good listener, and he had a wonderful knack of acknowledging individual change team members' contributions and he was totally unswerving in his commitment to the change programme. His success in this role led to a main board appointment in Taverns.

The change team also comprised five other Bass members and their key tasks ultimately included co-ordination of the activities of 11 project teams with 73 full-time members across the whole company. The team roles were:

- project management at the highest level
- benefits monitors
- new reward patterns
- internal and external communication
- implementation
- training
- HR management
- managing the board
- managing the consultants and contracts
- managing information requirements
- 'making it happen'.

The main project team's backgrounds were as varied as their ages and length of service:

IT Projects Manager – early 40s, male, marketing services experience, MBA, market researcher, former oil industry geologist, consumer expert and the change team sceptic and detailed planner and monitor.

Communications Manager – early 30s, female, former commercial manager, controller of the company newspaper and also most other media as well as being the public face of change.

Training and Implementation Project Manager – early 50s, male, MBA, worked for three other brewers, 30+ years in the industry, the organisation development thinker, background largely in operations, the team writer and theorist.

HR and Rewards Project Manager – early 40s, female, former personnel director, operational bias, expertise in employee relations and remuneration. Involved from the laboratory phase in BPR. Good team player and communicator – an operational realist.

Administration Co-ordinator – key player, female, 40s, former senior secretary, the real team co-ordinator. Played a key role in resource monitoring and internal company systems and 'keeping us sane and sensible'.

This was a phenomenally successful team who attained demanding goals. Human resource management specialists figured significantly in the team, emphasising the importance of people management to achievement of the objectives.

In addition to the Bass employee members of the main team there were, at the start, five consultants. It was recognised in Bass' case that external help would be needed. It was a wise decision. The consultants, from CSC Index, gave us a much-needed kick-start. They provided tools to help identify the options, tools to manage the project(s) reliably and tools to help us manage the process. The leader of the consultancy team, through prior acquaintance, also had the ear of the chief executive and this was a channel of communication that the change team frequently used. CSC also brought to the company expert knowledge in respect of information systems trends and new project management methodologies.

One key aspect of this nexus of relationships is to decide when the consultants are no longer needed and to plan the exit route for them and then implement it. In terms of bench-marking, CSC Index introduced us to a range of their clients and contacts against whom and with whom we could readily establish benchmarking networks.

The Leicester Royal Infirmary – Bringing the team together

What is the profile of a good re-engineering project leader?

The experiences of re-engineering at The Leicester Royal Infirmary have shown that a broad spectrum of skills and attributes is required from those leading the redesign efforts. Above all, re-engineering leaders have to be credible within the organisation and able to operate at all levels and be well respected by both clinical and managerial colleagues. It is difficult for someone from outside the hospital, however capable, to assume this type of role without a considerable lead time. Our shopping list of characteristics required for re-engineering leadership is as follows:

- [ ] vision – always with a mind on the desired outcome and always one step ahead
- [ ] divergent thinker – able to conceptualise widely but at the same time 'see the wood from the trees'
- [ ] creativity and ability to generate innovative solutions
- [ ] enthusiasm
- [ ] energy – relentless, doesn't give up easily, supports others through highs and lows
- [ ] able to manage within the political power structure
- [ ] risk taker
- [ ] ability to listen
- [ ] team player, able to relate to others at all levels
- [ ] sense of humour.

Interestingly, the entire process leadership team of The Leicester Royal Infirmary re-engineering programme is female. This appears to support an observation by Dr Michael Hammer that women are assuming an increasing number of re-engineering leadership roles. Typical 'female' attributes such as a coaching and facilitative approach, listening and supporting are appropriate for this role.

What is the profile of a good re-engineering team member?

The 'person specification' for an effective re-engineering team member has evolved as the programme has developed. Initially, much effort was made to ensure that team members represented a cross section of people from all levels who worked on the process being redesigned. However, as we moved to pilot the redesigned processes, we found that team members who had been seconded from managerial or clinical leadership positions were better equipped to help implementation. The key factor was ability to influence and the confidence to work with (and challenge) senior colleagues across the organisation. Other important aspects include:

- knowledge of hospital processes from experience
- respected by colleagues, preferably on a hospital-wide basis
- skills in analysis and synthesis
- able to think 'out of the box' and form an opinion
- commitment and energy
- personal resilience
- brings experience of implementing change from a previous context or programme
- able to plan and organise own workload and use initiative
- being a team player.

Using re-engineering consultants

The support of external re-engineering consultants has considerably aided The Leicester Royal Infirmary re-engineering effort. Given that there was little previous experience of health-care re-engineering for this Trust to draw upon, the management consultants played a key role in supporting the 'journey into the unknown'.

The original specification for consultancy support stated that the re-engineering programme must be hospital-driven, rather than management-consultant driven. The role of the management consultants was to act as 'coaches' to the hospital re-engineering teams. The Leicester Royal Infirmary spoke to more than 30 companies offering consultancy support before the management consultant partners were selected. Their role can be summarised as:

- coaching re-engineering teams in analytical skills, problem solving, presentation skills and re-engineering skills
- coaching senior management in new management models and programme management
- challenging and encouraging teams to 'think the unthinkable'
- injecting new thinking to the teams based on their experience of other re-engineering programmes

- ☐ ensuring that momentum was maintained and highly challenging targets set
- ☐ driving teams to defeat obstacles to success.

However, a number of other issues were identified which have wide implications for organisations using management consultancy support for major change programmes.

Balance of support

The requirement was for the consultant to 'coach' and 'facilitate' The Leicester Royal Infirmary team and to ensure that challenging targets were delivered within very tight time-scales. In some ways the requirements conflict. It takes time for an appropriately balanced relationship to develop. Short-term results can be achieved with a consultancy-driven approach, but hospital re-engineering can only succeed in the long term if it is led by the staff who must implement and sustain the change.

Balance of activity

A marked feature of the methodology suggested by many of the management consultancy firms approached was a detailed analysis of current processes and performance. While a certain level of analysis is important, this has to balanced with the need for a concerted effort to create practical and visible change from the very beginning of the re-engineering programme. There is a danger that programmes may fail to create the required degree of momentum.

Deliverables

Baseline information about many hospital-wide processes was not readily available at the beginning of the re-engineering programme. This made the setting of improvement targets both for the re-engineering team and the management consultancy difficult. Target setting must be an iterative process; as analysis is completed and design concepts are tested, achievable goals can be set.

Named consultants

Success of the management consultancy depends more on the calibre of individual consultants than on the consultancy firm as a whole.

Rank Xerox – bringing the team together

The managing director, Fournier, set targets for 1996 in the four corporate priority areas of customer satisfaction, employee satisfaction, market share and return on assets. He wanted 100 per cent satisfied customers; employee satisfaction at benchmark level in every country in Europe – where benchmark means above the national norm. Finally he wanted return on assets of 18 per cent. These results could not be achieved through business as usual, but he allowed time for a well-developed response. These targets were broadly in two groupings:

1   Desired state

- Customer focused
- Flexible organisation, empowered people
- Benchmark growth and costs
- World-class distribution
- Customer delight

2   Business targets

	1993	*1996*
Customer satisfaction	91 per cent	100 per cent
Employee satisfaction	Country norm	Benchmark
Market share	Current	Leadership
Return on assets	7 per cent	18 per cent

Fournier set up two design teams. The notional design of such teams had been developed in the early 1980s. Rank Xerox had developed participative problem solving to a high degree, and any form of top-down direction would have been unacceptable. The first team to report (actually known as Team B), recommended radical changes in International Headquarters, reducing its role in managing operating companies, simplifying and cutting central costs. The more difficult problem lay in the operating company structure in 15 European countries, where the organisation and management methods still bore strong similarities to the original Rank Xerox structure set up in the 1960s. The new European design was developed by Team A, with managers from across the company. (Team C, to be set up in 1993, concentrated further on growth.) Team A comprised line managers from six countries and from all important functions, including HRM, communications, customer service, finance, quality, information management, and process management.

These were well-respected people, with broad experience in the company; the line managers were from successful operations, and all had worked on team problem solving at international level. They brought experience with self-managed work groups, process design, and good analytical and communications skills. As in the 1980s, the role of consultants was minimal; there was discussion with the management school at INSEAD, often used by Rank Xerox for management development. INSEAD provided valuable models for 'conversion levels' of product streams to market sectors to geography, but the main body of the design was initiated by Rank Xerox.

Royal Bank of Scotland – bringing the team together

In 1991, the newly created Branch Banking Division was given a new managing director, Tony Schofield. The chief executive George Mathewson had recognised Schofield as having the insight, drive and ambition to help him achieve the vision of building 'The best performing Financial Services Institution by 1997'.

Unlike many of his new executive colleagues, Schofield had spent his entire career with the bank. Shrewdly, Mathewson recognised that while dramatic change was necessary, he still had a business to run. The changes had to take place without alienating customers or staff. Schofield had worked in the Bank all his life; he knew where the skeletons of organisational dysfunction were buried, but under the previous leadership he had been discouraged from taking action. However, he knew that the need to improve profit was imperative. This could only be achieved by removing the cross-subsidy of products, charging an economic and competitive price for each product and driving the costs down. Some hard decisions had to be made. His new Division employed 16,000, had a geographically dispersed network of 750 branches that stretched from the

Shetlands to Cornwall, poor infrastructure and massive bad debts. Prior to Schofield's appointment in March 1991, a small 'skunk works' team working under the direction of the chief executive had undertaken an analysis of the ills, which they had identified as:

- organisational design
- quality of key people
- lack of vision and under investment in IT culminating in the technologists determining priorities and projects
- unreliable lending and pricing policies
- unimaginative products.

To the casual observer, this could have been considered somewhat perverse, particularly when Direct Line (at the time best known for its imaginative and successful all-out assault on the UK car insurance market) was part of the Royal Bank Group. Unlike the core banking business, Direct Line was led by a visionary leader in Peter Wood, who knew his business could only function and reinvent the insurance market if it was completely autonomous and unencumbered by the structures and culture of the old bank.

Schofield took the core of Mathewson's 'skunk works' team to become the catalyst for his change programme. He appointed as project leader Cameron McPhail, who had joined the bank two years earlier to work in the group strategy function. McPhail has a PhD in economics and a MBA. Furthermore, he had spent a number of years in California as the Scottish Development Agency's representative in San Francisco. At the time of his appointment in March 1992, McPhail had never managed a significant number of people; however, by the time he moved on from the core change programme in 1995 to re-engineer the bank's off-shore businesses as chief executive, he led a change team that at its peak would number 300.

In conventional wisdom, McPhail would have been a risky appointment – he had no general management experience, had never been a banker, furthermore his experience outside the bank had been limited to being a 'Salesman for Scotland' to generate inward investment from corporate America. What he did have, however, was a huge intellect, enormous powers of analysis, passion for change and an unflinching resolve to help George Mathewson and managing director Schofield achieve their vision.

The appointment of the change programme leader was an early critical step that would set the tone for what was to follow. By thinking 'outside the box' in appointing McPhail, the project agenda was firmly set, it was not going to be a case of 'successfully managing change, while maintaining the *status quo*'.

A programme of scale and magnitude could not be successfully implemented without the twin resources of people and time. An early decision was taken to appoint a major consultancy firm to the change team. What the bank didn't have, the consultants could provide in abundance, particularly their experience of process redesign, large project management methodologies, together with a reputation for radical thinking and an ability to challenge assumptions. Even more critical was the realisation by the key players that to achieve the changes necessary for corporate success would require continuous change. There was no panacea, an environment and appetite for continuous change and organisational renewal had to be built, together with the skill set to ensure success.

The decision to surround the consultants with specialists from the bank who were seconded into the project full time was the key to establishing effective technology transfer between the consultants and the bank. Furthermore, in the medium to long term, it would provide the business with the skills necessary for continuous change. In addition, by dedicating significant numbers of employees to the programme, it was a clear demonstration of organisational commitment that it wanted fundamental and impactful change and was prepared to invest resources to achieve its goals.

Toshiba – bringing the team together

What was to be addressed was not just a project relating to part of an organisation but a fundamental organisational redesign. With the incredibly tight time-scale in which the organisation had to be redesigned it was considered that those involved in the design should be those who would have to make the processes work on an ongoing basis. There was little pressure from the parent company to involve outside 'experts', consultants and the like in the initial stages. Indeed, had external consultants been used, by the time these had been selected and briefed, half the project time available might have been used up. Nevertheless, novel ideas that were developed were 'tested out' against external expert opinion before being incorporated into a final proposal.

In the event, the team comprised a mix of individuals who would manage the new operation, key managers seconded temporarily from the Rank Organisation who had been involved in the joint venture, one specialist from the parent company and the chairman of the parent company who adopted an intimate watching brief role rather than day-to-day involvement with all the detailed considerations. All of the members needed to have an understanding of the particular requirements for manufacturing televisions, a 'quality mentality' and a capacity for selfless dedication to the task in hand, virtually round the clock. Three main processes had been identified:

☐ assembling televisions
☐ managing systems
☐ managing people.

These had been identified before the team set-up, drawing from experience within the joint venture and relying heavily upon the production engineering and systems experience of Toshiba in Japan. Production engineering processes and a new production and material control process from Japan were to be adopted as 'givens'. Toshiba was, world-wide, a leading television manufacturer and knew technically how to make televisions better than most. Its design and manufacturing technology was in the forefront of the best companies in the world. What would be different in the UK would be the people processes and the processes for procurement of local materials. It was in these areas that the project team would have to concentrate in order to realise the manufacturing and systems potentials.

The choice of project leader was not perhaps so much inspired as obvious. Geoffrey Deith had become managing director of the joint venture company (management had been vested with Rank Organisation) some six months beforehand and had displayed considerable leadership skills, business acumen and a sensitivity and capability in dealing with people matters. The personnel director of the joint venture company knew the people issues on site intimately and would be a vital bridge; he was also temporarily seconded from the Rank Organisation. For the ongoing top team, some interesting choices were made. The production director, an engineer by training, had spent most of his working life in quality management. The person who would become the materials director had mainly a computing background, latterly as systems manager of the joint venture company. The finance director had been a middle-ranking company accountant, recognised somewhat as a 'young Turk'. The engineering director, as earlier mentioned, had been the technical director in the joint venture company and formerly chief engineer of Toshiba Corporation's main television factory in Japan. Wider human resource management issues and legal matters were covered by the parent company's director of personnel. The team was completed by the parent company's chairman.

The chairman astutely said that selection of the team had more to do with art than science. These key appointments were nevertheless thought through most carefully in an endeavour to get the right mix of capability and attitude. All were 'known quantities', having each worked in the joint venture company and/or the parent company. All were selected as being able to bring the very best that was available irrespective of previous status and functional responsibility. Prime among the considerations was the 'attitude' of the individuals, all of whom were able to display high levels of intellect, flexibility and tenacity coupled with appropriate technical capabilities. Most had considerable people-management experience and more than a third were either practising HR professionals or had had considerable personnel-related experience.

While never a member directly of the planning team, Roy Sanderson, national organiser for the Electrical, Electronic, Telecommunications and Plumbing Trade Union (EETPU), ultimately became an effective and creative contributor to the planning process. He had personally extensively researched management thinking and processes of Japanese high technology companies and was sensitive to their objectives. He was also one of the prime movers in his Union to find a 'new way' for industrial relations in the UK. The value of his contribution cannot be underestimated. His involvement heralded a new level of co-operation between UK companies and that Union. He had gained the backing of his general secretary but it was unquestionably his personal resolve, sensitivity and tenacity that made the difference in the Toshiba case. The outcome was a new partnership which has endured for more than a decade.

The project team then had a charismatic leader with very wide commercial experience and particular people sensitivities, with other members being dedicated professionals from a wide variety of representative functions; all of them willing to commit to finding new solutions in response to a considerable challenge.

4

PREPARING AND MOVING FORWARD

□ Successful initiatives do not focus on cost-down or people downsizing.

□ People-related systems, individual attitudes and organisational climate must all change.

□ Managing insecurity is critical; safety valves have to be designed and be put in place.

□ Involvement, at the right stage, of all those affected, will pay valuable dividends.

□ Training for transition is necessary.

□ Considerable, multifaceted, communication is vital.

Brainstorming of one kind or another is a consistent feature of preparation activity in all BPR initiatives. For success, such activity cannot be undertaken lightly or in haste. Initial scoping studies to identify the biggest opportunities for change have taken some of the best teams weeks and months; and that's with the very best people working flat out, full time. They may be working from a strategic vision expressed by someone or might genuinely be starting with absolutely a blank page.

Initial focus

In the case of Rank Xerox who had been undergoing extensive quality and organisational change programmes for a number of years, the initial focus was upon return on assets employed, not just in the UK but across Europe; so their starting point, while specific, was far-ranging in its implications and caused them to go to the core of all their operating procedures. Assets employed have few boundaries. Indeed they couldn't start without considerable information being brought to hand through a rigorous process of benchmarking. Leadership vision identified priority monitoring areas of customer satisfaction, employee satisfaction, market share and return on assets; what might be described as the 'challenge from the chief executive', which was passed down to individual countries but with an overall team from managers across the company representing line management from six countries. All important functions were represented, including HRM, communications, service quality, information management and lastly their internal consultancy-type function, process management.

In all the other organisations within this study there was similar representation. Notable is that none of the case studies solely focused on cost-down and people downsizing which is erroneously considered by many outsiders of BPR to be either the main purpose or the main outcome. In Bass Tavern's case they were being caused to be much smaller through external intervention and having, by Government decree (of the way that the brewery business was to be organised in the UK) to divest themselves of nearly half their public houses. So the opportunity, if anything, was for growth through efficiency. The focus of all the studies has been on solutions for the longer term so that even if, in order to get somewhere, downsizing was required, the concept was that the outcome should provide for the capability for (a) at least survival and (b) a step-change in the quality of the services provided, and that the generation of new ideas and opportunities might present new opportunities for growth.

Involving people

The make-up of the team mentioned in Chapter 3 is vital to the outcome. Not only does a vision have to be translated into a notion of design, that design has to be refined to be practical, and to provide the desired outputs. The means have to be put in place to bring this to successful realisation and viable ongoing operation. All of these elements require consideration of the human factors. People are the ones that have got to make it work and people, if not inclined, have the capacity to ensure that it doesn't work. To ignore the people issues is to ensure failure. People issues have to be considered for and by the starting team.

Whatever outcomes are to be achieved the best outcomes are likely to arise through thorough analysis and consideration, and 'agreement' of all of the operations and functional experts who will be accountable for the design. And the design needs to include the way that the new processes will roll out and be embedded.

Think 'implementation' early

While all the cases illustrated in this book can be said to be successful, not one of them does not admit to a view that they could, at the design stage, have done much more thinking about the implementation process. All of them gave considerable attention to communications. But the best one-way communications in the world are not enough to bring about voluntary change in people's attitudes and behaviour. The only kind that will work will be indoctrination, and that goes against the principles of BPR.

Productive learning

What has to take place throughout the enterprise is a process of 'productive learning'. This can be said to take place when new knowledge and new tasks run into and merge with the learners' activity and previous knowledge. It is therefore an integrative process and requires a minimisation or absence of conditions which would work against attainment of the desired objectives. If there are to be conditions that work against the desired objectives, these must be addressed. Productive learning involves close merging of knowledge, skills and attitudes.

The top team is most likely to experience productive learning. All of the team's combined knowledge, skills and attitudes will need to be put under scrutiny. Assumptions that have been held dear will be caused to be reviewed. Viewpoints born out of years of experience and embedded behaviour will be caused to be challenged. It is in these areas that external facilitators are being shown to be able to provide tools that more safely enable assumptions to be re-examined. Michael Hammer, after some years of examining the ins and outs of change management in the context of business process re-engineering, observes: 'Change coupled with management is about people's feelings and in re-engineering everyone feels like ****!' If you don't have a process that can safely address the issues arising out of people's feelings, through the start processes right through to implementation, then prospects of success will be severely undermined.

Knowing where you're going

Starting, with business process re-engineering, is also about knowing where you will be finishing. Knowing where you will be finishing includes anticipating and planning to either go through or around or to disassemble the barriers that will inevitably arise. The barriers in each case will vary by each organisation. Research has shown that certain difficulties are common to most organisations and that these follow a pattern in terms of degree of difficulty. Business Intelligence concluded, in rank order of difficulty, the following barriers in re-engineering business processes:

1   Managing change.
2   Developing multi-functional team competencies.
3   Establishing the process and managing support responsibilities.
4   Developing support systems.
5   Identifying process boundaries.[34]

The elements for change

This book is not about the techniques for undertaking the detailed technical analysis and design of business processes, but about the people elements. In all of the above barriers, people issues are at the forefront. Change in re-engineered organisations occurs at three levels:

☐ Changing the various organisational systems from work

design, reporting and working relationships through to reward systems etc.

☐ Changing the individuals who work in the organisation, their skills, values, attitudes and behaviour.

☐ Changing the organisational climate and how people work together, how open people are with each other, how decisions are made and how difficulties and conflicts are resolved, etc.

The means to change

In a model for change developed by Kurt Lewin, a pioneer in the field of social psychology of organisations, the initial step of any change process is to 'unfreeze' the existing pattern of behaviour as a means to managing resistance to change.[35] At the design stage this can be translated into providing a freeing-up of minds to creatively address issues. Accepting Lewin's model, 'unfreezing' needs to take place at each of the three levels and needs to start with the initial team itself. The individuals within it, the concept of the team's roles and the climate and interpersonal styles, translating into how they work together. Each of the members in the design team need to address consciously and unconsciously the need for change and become aware of their own behaviour patterns, to make them more open to the change process. In this aspect alone, external facilitators can be extremely valuable.

In Lewin's second step of movement, which involves making the actual changes that will bring about the organisation operating at a different level, there will be a need for people to behave quite differently and demonstrate new skills and processes. At the structural level, the organisation will inevitably change shape; supporting relationships in what might become a much more decentralised organisation with 'empowered' individuals and groups, will fundamentally change ... and the climate and interpersonal styles within the organisation will be subject to considerable modification. During this stage of change, Lewin indicates implicitly the need for greater levels of interpersonal trust and openness and fewer dysfunctional interactions.

The final stage of Lewin's change model relates to 'refreezing';

involving the stabilisation or institutionalisation that 'normalise' the changes that have occurred. These will require new structures to be put in place to ensure the maintenance, for example ensuring that new recruits into the organisation share the organisation's management style and value systems. Critical to this process, if not otherwise addressed earlier, will be that the reward systems actually reinforce the behaviours in an integrated and orderly way.

Here is a different way to express the phases of change, which to an extent translates Lewin's concepts into different elements:

☐ mobilising resources
☐ analysing processes
☐ discovering ways forward
☐ verifying workability
☐ implementing the outcomes
☐ realising the benefits.

All these phases will involve feelings and behaviours of:

☐ denial that anything needs to be done
☐ shock that something needs to be done or will be done
☐ resistance if for no other reason than people feel comfortable with 'the known'
☐ acceptance that something will change and realisation of their 'lot' in that change (most likely thinking the worst)
☐ adoption of at least the bare model for the re-engineered process
☐ commitment to the processes and embedded acceptance of the new processes as a norm.

Anticipating resistance

Anticipating behavioural resistance to change is fundamental to preparing people for the process of change. This difficulty has been recognised for a long time but is still the major obstacle on which organisations founder in carrying through change. Machiavelli, in his famous book *The Prince*, said: 'There is nothing more difficult to take in hand, more perilous to conduct, or more uncertain of success than to take a lead in the introduction of a new order of things, because the innovation has for enemies all those who have done well under the old conditions and lukewarm defenders in those who may do well under the new.' This prophetic statement captures the essence of the difficulties of bringing about major re-engineered change and a new order of things in our age. Resistance can take many forms:

☐ Rejection ('There is nothing wrong that a minor adjustment to X wouldn't put right')
☐ Procrastination ('We'll do that tomorrow but today ...')
☐ Indecision ('We need to give this further consideration ...')
☐ Lack of implementation follow-up (paralysis by analysis)
☐ Strategic ineffectiveness ('The more products we sell the more money we lose')
☐ Sabotage ('What the eye doesn't see the heart won't grieve over')
☐ Regression ('Let's forget these wild ideas and get back to real work ...')

Counter-resistance strategies

Ansoff has suggested a firm's strategic response to its environment will be more timely and effective if capability is developed in conjunction with a new strategy.[36] Performance will hopefully be more effective after the capability is installed. The process of capability installation more than doubles the workload, and the rise and changes in culture and the impact on individual power-bases becomes more visible. As a result, even higher resistance will be experienced. But if these issues are not addressed at the planning stage by all of the planning team, then as a minimum the resources necessary to address them will not be provided for and the viability of implementing the newly emerging processes will be undermined. These issues have been known about and recognised for centuries. The Chinese warlord Sun Tzu in his work, *The Art of War*, includes amongst his six principles, 'match target with resources'. The others are: concentrate, surprise, choose ground, ensure communication and innovate. These, too, have some relevance to BPR!

The writer of the Bass Taverns case study, Gordon Steven, has observed 'Where change meets culture head-on, culture always wins'. But it depends how quickly and how clearly the strength of the new culture is envisioned and to what extent processes are put in place to bring about cultural change. Without them, as Gordon has observed, the original culture will surely override the new changes.

Individuals will resist change when it makes them feel insecure or when their position of power or authority is threatened. It is pretty certain that the scale of change brought about by BPR will be considerable. Groups will resist change in proportion to the extent they find their powers as a group threatened and where the changes violate accepted values and norms and are based either upon information which the group regards as irrelevant or on a model of reality which differs from the model held to be valid by the group. The design process for change must take into account these issues. Ansoff proposes that the ground should be prepared in advance through a series of measures aimed at:

- [ ] minimising start-up resistance
- [ ] marshalling a power base to give momentum and continuity
- [ ] preparing a plan for the change process which assigns responsibilities, resources, steps and interactions, through which the change will be carried out
- [ ] designing into the planned behavioural features, which will optimise the acceptance and support for the new facilities and capabilities.

Achieving balance

Nick Obolensky, in his excellent book *Practical Business Process Re-engineering*, usefully illustrates a matrix developed within Signa Corporation in the USA together with Symmetrix, a Boston-based consultancy.[37] In this matrix, teams start from a chaotic level with ambiguous goals and processes, new faces and lots of questions. The matrix suggests a move from there against two dimensions: high relationship focus centred on social needs, where confrontation is avoided and where there is a good spirit but little action; compared with a high task focus centred on doing ('just to it!') with limited co-operation, good action but poor spirit. The optimum is to achieve a balance between the high relationship focus and the high task focus in what is described as the 'true team', where there is good performance against tasks, the team and individuals are happy, there is mutual respect, good achievement of objectives and generally a good spirit. That is the kind of balance needed to be achieved within organisations; between the relationships on the one hand and operational tasks on the other. Imbalance will undermine the capability to perform to optimum levels.

As regards bringing the team together, the stages are 'forming', 'storming', 'norming' and 'performing'. If the team is made up of new faces then this process will certainly have to be gone through in one way or another.

Creating a supportive climate

A supportive climate has to be engineered. Misconceptions and exaggerations need to be eliminated by making clear the needs or opportunities, and the beneficial consequences of the change. Fears and anxieties should be made clear to groups and individuals of positive and negative impacts of the change upon them. To the extent possible, changes can be made in the power structure which will increase the power behind the change through forming coalitions of those who are very 'pro' and enlisting so far 'lukewarm' supporters. Rewards can be offered for supporting the change, not necessarily monetary.

Marginalise opposition

To the extent possible, individuals or groups who are perceived to continue to resist the change need to be excluded. This is not a proposal that debates the morality of a particular issue, merely the effectiveness of actions that will be necessary. Those individuals who will be involved in implementing the change should be included in the decision making that will relate to the change.

Plan for quick delivery

Contrary to other declarations, this book asserts that change should be contained over the shortest possible time. Where possible, starts should always be made with groups that are committed to the change and can see the benefits; they should be recognised and rewarded and then the change spread to other units. 'We want some of that ...' is an ideal. No assumption should be made that managers and others have the necessary knowledge and skills to deal with things that are entirely novel to them. Learning processes must be built in and, as commented upon above, the climate for learning must be created.

Overcome passive resistance

As well as active resistance to change, passive resistance, perhaps related to incapability, is a form of opposition which has to be overcome. Minimising such resistance can be helped by providing dedicated resources, assigning time as well as money. For example, integrate management development programmes into the change process by integrating the change issues as exercises. To the extent possible, concentrate investment on behaviour development which can then be linked to systems build-up towards strategic actions.

Overcome systemic resistance

Systemic resistance to change occurs when operating and strategic activities within an organisation compete for capacity. Unless provisions are made, normal operating work will tend to pre-empt strategic work. For that reason the total dedication on a 100 per cent allocation basis of the top team is virtually a prerequisite.

Produce support and resistance 'maps'

Leaving things to chance, or general assumption, is inadequate. An analysis needs to be recorded, perhaps against the existing organisation chart, which will highlight the support and resistance areas, such as: the extent of political/cultural disturbance which will occur in the affected units, or the key individuals who are thought will support or resist change.

Kick-starting

Getting teams to work effectively together towards structured and focused objectives is the role of leadership and the province of specialist facilitators. Bringing teams together in different ways calls for different leadership strategies than many leaders have hitherto experienced. It takes time to shake down a team but, usually, within business process re-engineering, time is at an absolute premium (it should be at other times too!). This book is not about the techniques of teambuilding and effective teamworking, but if teams are not effective then the aims and objectives of the organisation cannot be achieved, certainly within the parameters set down. Kick-starting the team and bringing all necessary issues into focus has been the remit of a number of consultancies supporting cases illustrated in this book. Bass, The Leicester Royal Infirmary and Royal Bank of Scotland each assert that they would not have been able to move forward at the pace that they did without the support of external specialists. These issues are considered in Chapter 4.

Roles for HR specialists

Internal specialists, particularly human resource specialists who should know the particular workings of an organisation in relation to its people, have a vital role to play. The following checklist is provided for guidance:

1   Putting 'safety valves' in place before starting, including planning reassignment and exit processes and mechanisms to support some of the stressful situations that will inevitably arise.
2   Working at the heart of communications initiatives. The Bass case study particularly highlights this.
3   Developing and defining core competencies for new jobs as they emerge, and determining and supporting the recruitment and selection processes for them both for internal or external appointments.
4   Reviewing and revising performance management and reward processes and systems.
5   Developing selection and rejection criteria and the mechanisms necessary to apply them including acquisition of new skills and sensitivities by individuals.
6   Helping determine the cultural and the support and resistance 'maps' of the organisation and the planning of the

strategies to deal with them. Capitalising upon the positive contributions and developing processes to override, go round or change the nature of opposition.

7 Benchmarking people factors across their own organisation and against other organisations.

8 Developing and managing role and transition training programmes.

9 Re-engineering their own functional roles relative to the needs of the emerging requirements of the whole organisation.

10 Ensuring that all of the human resource management systems relating to relationships with employees, employee training and development, employee resourcing and reward, are compatible with each other and are mutually supportive and are also compatible with the needs of the organisation.

11 Facilitating learning, facilitating learning, facilitating learning (*ad infinitum*!).

12 Contributing, as members of the team, to the wider operational competitive and customer related needs.

Fundamental choices for HR practitioners

Human resource practitioners have, in relation to business process re-engineering, a number of choices:

☐ Wait for things to happen.

☐ Resist interference with their roles.

☐ Follow visionary line management blindly.

☐ Hide and hope it will all go away.

Or ...

☐ Learn everything there is to know about change and relate that to their own organisation.

☐ Partner their line manager and other functional manager colleagues in finding new ways that span all functions.

☐ Lead in the identification of all the people-related needs, providing solutions to difficulties before they arise.

☐ Practise what they preach and help deliver rather than just talk about change.

Contingencies and costs

All of the other points relate firstly to the primary change team but also to other teams that roll out through the process of change. Whether the scheme of things is designed at the centre and rolled out in one go, as with Toshiba, or whether there are a series of redesigned processes and re-engineering laboratories, each successfully dealing with a major whole aspect of change as with The Leicester Royal Infirmary, the principles hold good. A new addage is 'When the "'go" button is pressed, all contingencies should have been provided for ... especially the unknown ones!'

Every project will have unknown contingencies. It's difficult to put a budgetary figure on it but if there's been considerable attention to identifying and planning, then between 30 and 70 per cent of the costs already planned for should be provided as a contingency. Another rule of thumb offered by Bass is that for every £1,000 you spend on planning you will need to spend at least 10 times that on implementation. Starting again is just as expensive as starting up from scratch ... or more so.

Bass Taverns – preparing and moving forward

Bass started with a team of 12 executives being locked away for four months with a team of five consultants from CSC Index to literally start all over again. They developed the strategic vision of the chief executive officer into a series of capability needs and requirements. They developed the new plans, the redesigns rooted in the newly identified core processes. This led onto simulated laboratory trials, field pilots and then into roll out, over roughly a two-year time-scale. All the way through these phases of BPR we had internal and external benchmarking and measurement of hard and soft data at every step. Attitude surveys were just as important to us as hard costings. We linked the *Strategic Vision* of being Britain's No. 1 Pub Retailer to our capabilities, by focusing on the core processes. These were, from the preliminary work, defined as (a) operate pubs, (b) develop pubs, (c) manage cash. And we attained top management commitment to the strategic vision as well as the core processes. It was then a relatively simple step to re-organise the company around the three core processes.

Some special issues can be highlighted. One is, customer focus is key. One of our change projects was called 'Succeeding with Customers' and it was our total quality initiative in the pubs involving our retail staff. At the same time, we launched our corporate total quality management initiative for staff and managers who worked in our regional offices and our head office. Customers became real in the minds of the men and women who worked for us whether internal or external customers. This acknowledges the fact that while all the other core change initiatives were taking place and contrary to what BPR purists might recommend, we were still interested and committed towards incremental improvement in everything we did. BPR was producing the radical shift in performance, TQM was producing incremental improvement. We saw in these nothing but complementary activity. What TQM did for us was to highlight the fact that 'we are all customers now' and we must be the purveyors of quality goods and services.

Our way of dealing with sceptics and cynics was direct: sack the latter and convince the former! You do really have to care for the wounded but shoot the stragglers! There is no room for cynics; we concluded that if you are not with change then you are against it! A big danger to be recognised was what could be described as 'malevolent compliance'. Your communication antennae have to be especially sensitive to spot this behaviour.

There were particular roles and responsibilities for the HR specialists:

1   Communications. They had a special role in the communications processes; accepting ownership and editorial power over all channels of communication and optimising their use. In the change team we once worked out that we had used over 20 different methods of communicating and that human resource practitioners controlled or significantly influenced all of them. They are:

Bridge screen	Message on all PCs and workstations
Newspaper, *Inn Touch*	Total editorial control
Press visits to pubs	Significant control
Audio tapes	Significant control
Company videos	Significant control

Company-wide presentations	Significant control
Company core brief from the board	Significant control
Regional company conferences	Always contributed
National company conferences	Total production and content control
IT newsletter	Had a column
Property newsletter	Had a column
Operations newsletter	Had a column
Messages in pay slips	Total control
Franking message – internal	Total control
Franking message – external	Total control
Friday gossip column	An E-mail message every Friday on serious and not so serious items – widely responded to by all areas
Sporting event/entertaining	Took key internal and external customers on follow-up visits and presentations
E-mail	Extensive use was made of this facility in Taverns and other divisions.
Plc relations	Presentations were made to our key stakeholders in Bass plc.
National conferences (external)	Presentations were made at the IPD National Conference and others, from Microsoft in Seattle to Mercedes-Benz in Germany to the Cabinet Office in Peterborough.

This list of communication channels highlights the depth and breadth of our attempts to communicate. The list does not cover the constant face-to-face communications that took place (one to one and group), nor does it include any detail or considerations of the input we made to the designs or implementation of training courses, which was substantial. HR was at the heart of all communication initiatives.

2   Managing entry and re-entry of project staff into the business operations. This includes moving 'perceived' wisdom from views such as ... 'Oh, she is just on a project', to a perspective of 'She is heading for better things, she is heading up one of those change projects'. That is a central issue for entry and if you attain this goal then we perceive you have fewer or no problems in the re-entry of your team into the business when the project, as such, is complete. When we started, we were faced with recruits demanding a guarantee of re-entry or at worst their old job back. This has long since gone. Why? Because, of the 11 original project managers, five have been promoted to general management posts, two have switched projects and five of the originals remain.

It has to be acknowledged that a key role for the BPR team leader is the management and development of his team. Our BPR project managers are change champions – they would not be successful unless they embraced change. They can manage projects. They can manage interdisciplinary, cross-functional teams. They can manage resources and they can deliver. Therefore, they have a lot of general management skills which are in demand in most organisations.

3   Core competencies in the new jobs are critical. We have just mentioned project management skills, positive attitudes toward change, etc., but we perceive that these have to be refined in the jobs within the core processes. In our own case, we redefined the pivotal jobs in the core processes of operate pubs, develop pubs and manage cash. One key element from our experience is the ability to manage information along the core process and to adopt or design such information systems. The obvious issue for HR then becomes, do you reward on the basis of core competencies?

4   Redesigning reward packages – most of our re-engineering work in Bass Taverns has resulted in the formation of teams to tackle operational or development opportunities. This has demanded addressing team as well as individual-related pay.

5   Empowerment and transition training – there can never be enough of either. Our new retailing initiative programme has, at its heart, a substantial role change for the area managers who are responsible for a number of pubs, and not inconsiderable empowerment for the pub managers. Empowerment is a difficult word or concept outside the particulars of your own company and its people. What could be said in Bass is that it has been the role of HR to make empowerment meaningful. Our concept has been 'How will you get Managers to act in powerful and new ways?' The heart of the answer for us was quite simple – give them something powerful and meaningful to do. In the case of Bass Taverns licensed house managers, they are empowered to appoint their own people, they are empowered to develop their own pricing policies to deliver budgeted gross profits, they are empowered to devise and implement promotional plans for their outlets. They, then, feel empowered to make these things happen and just do it. These are the most powerful decisions that can be made in a pub. The accountabilities are integrated and indivisible.

6   Role and transition training. The content of role and transition training programmes follows readily and easily from the empowerment matrix outlined above. Licensed house managers have to be competent in selection and training, finance and pricing policy, promotional support, product mix, etc. The only thing to add is confidence and often this comes from working in a team.

Knowing when to press the 'go' button, for Bass, was no problem. We recognised that we had the board behind us. We had the best possible team available and we felt confident. We had honestly endeavoured to meet every foreseeable contingency and we had identified the core processes and the cutting-edge competencies. We had considered everything in a totally holistic way. We needed to go for it and we needed what we described as a series of quick hits. When it happened, there was plenty of shouting about the success that followed.

The Leicester Royal Infirmary – preparing and moving forward

Preparing people for the process
Following nearly 12 months of research, planning and communication, The Leicester Royal Infirmary re-engineering programme commenced formally in May 1994 with a month-long 'scoping study'. A core group of clinical and managerial staff led a process to:

- [ ] identify the biggest opportunities for change
- [ ] harness the ideas and enthusiasms of key internal and external players for the re-engineering programme
- [ ] determine the strategic positioning of the programme as a means to achieving the strategic direction
- [ ] identify the initial process map, programme plan and time-scales.

Establishing re-engineering laboratory teams
The design phase commenced in August 1994 with the establishment of three re-engineering laboratory teams. A re-engineering laboratory is a physical facility in which to test ideas and accelerate learning. A re-engineering laboratory team is a group of five to seven people seconded full time from their normal jobs, who analyse an existing process and redesign and test its replacement. The Leicester Royal Infirmary was one of the first healthcare organisations to adopt this way of working. An evaluation of the re-engineering laboratory approach identified the following advantages:

- [ ] High degree of focus – team members have the opportunity to concentrate on the change process, rather than balance it with operational responsibilities. This creates considerable momentum for change.
- [ ] Validation – concepts are thoroughly tested before change takes place within the organisation so that many of the issues arising in implementation are anticipated in advance.

☐ Team work – enabling cross-functional teams to resolve their problems on a process level has been extremely valuable. Doctors, clerks and nurses involved in re-engineering patient processes have all commented on the value of meeting together to develop a common view of the issues involved.

☐ Scope – concentrating on 'end to end' processes, across the hospital, has broadened the potential to create and sustain change.

☐ Personal growth – re-engineering laboratory team members involved in the changes have risen to challenges in a way that has exceeded expectations. This has benefited both the hospital and the individual.

Many issues identified in the early phases of the programme have been amended:

☐ Implementation – in the early phases of the re-engineering process, from analysis to design concept, the work was led by the laboratory teams. Staff in the hospital who were responsible for implementation were frequently not deeply involved in the process until pilots were developed. As the re-engineering programme has evolved, ownership and involvement has been enhanced by bringing in identified implementers from the start of each laboratory.

☐ Staff secondment – staff selected for re-engineering laboratory team membership are among the 'brightest and best' in the organisation. Tensions are inevitably created when such people are removed from key roles in the day-to-day operations of the hospital. In this context, senior management sponsorship of the programme is crucial. Appropriate cover arrangements must be established and a careful overview maintained.

☐ Re-entry strategy – re-engineering laboratory team membership has been described as 'five years of personal development packed into six months'. There is a problem in relocating team members into their previous jobs, in terms of their expectations, possible lack of opportunity to make change in their operational roles and readjustment at the end of their secondment. Organisational 're-entry' of

secondees requires very special attention within a re-engineering programme.

☐ Liaison between re-engineering laboratory teams – interface
and interdependency between the re-engineered processes
requires high levels of co-ordination and co-operation. At
The Leicester Royal Infirmary, locating all teams in the
same venue (an old Victorian hospital ward) has brought
many benefits.

A re-engineering methodology for the NHS

The change management methodology describes a framework
and steps taken to bring about radical change. It is at the heart
of the re-engineering programme. The assimilated learning
from The Leicester Royal Infirmary suggests that generic
change management methodologies used successfully in industry must be modified for use in a healthcare environment. The
difficulties experienced in attempting to apply classic re-engineering methodologies at The Leicester Royal Infirmary
include:

☐ Early attempts to baseline and analyse existing operational
performance was time consuming and frustrating for the re-
engineering laboratory teams.

☐ Following analysis of existing processes, attempts were
made to 'vision' or conceptualise new ways of working.
Many clinical staff found the abstract discussions difficult
to relate to the practicalities of providing patient services.
They only became totally engaged in the process when new
services were actually being designed.

☐ Planning of implementation was difficult until the early
pilot results had been achieved.

☐ Design and implementation proved to be an iterative
process and difficult to plan in great detail at an early stage.

The unique challenges of the NHS healthcare environment
require a re-engineering methodology playing to the strengths
of the organisation. As The Leicester Royal Infirmary's initial
scoping study stated: 'The key ingredient is not some specific
project management method. It is people with ingredient and
imagination to anticipate the future implications of today's
decisions.'

A successful change management methodology has been developed. The baselining and visioning stages are kept to a minimum. The re-engineering laboratory team starts with an early hypothesis to provide a focus for a short analytical phase:

☐ Learning is achieved most effectively through implementation.

☐ Each aggregate patient group has different needs and each process must be implemented many times. For instance, a redesigned outpatient process has to be implemented for 350 clinics. Each clinic has unique features which have to be taken into account. Significant process variation is therefore required.

☐ Experience from each pilot is incorporated into the design of the next. Much effort is spent evaluating the learning and building it back into the programme. Consequently, a constant evaluation takes place.

☐ Lines of authority are complex and significant consensus building is required before big change can be implemented.

☐ However, the organisation is able to achieve change very rapidly once the change is defined and stakeholders agree.

Vital roles for personnel and development specialists
Human resource specialists have played a key role in the programme to date. They have:

☐ put a human resources framework into place before the programme commenced

☐ led key aspects of the communications initiatives

☐ led discussions with trade unions and professional groups

☐ advised on the human resource implications of all re-engineering initiatives

☐ developed and defined core competencies for new jobs

☐ advised on selection processes

☐ assessed new roles and redefined reward packages

☐ led the 'benefit realisation' aspect of the programme

☐ led the strategic development of an organisation-wide performance measurement framework

☐ led the strategy for the organisation-wide development of self-managed teams

☐ developed competency frameworks

☐ led training and development activities for new roles and responsibilities.

The nature of a re-engineering programme in an National Health Service context means that such a programme could not succeed without major human resources input and strong and visionary leadership at the head of that function.

Every aspect of the hospital's operation is under scrutiny from a re-engineering perspective. The programme makes many demands on the human resource function and has led it to question its own capacity to lead, support and facilitate the radical change. Although at an early stage, the human resource function is in the process of re-engineering itself, moving from a traditional functional view of human resource management. The aim is to integrate human resource management into the core operational processes of the hospital, playing a central role in building the capacity for change within the organisation.

Rank Xerox – preparing and moving forward

The scope of the redesign included both growth and cost reduction and it is important that cost reduction was not the sole objective. It was felt that this would lead to 'corporate anorexia' – being thin but not healthy. Capacity for growth was considered to be vitally important. The team was empowered with a virtually unlimited brief. It produced recommendations on decentralisation, empowerment and process redesign, which were all accepted. Downsizing was, of course, important but the team equally concentrated on style and culture – moving from command and control to coaching and counselling, as the way of running the company. It also acknowledged that national cultures vary across Europe, and that each region should have freedom to adapt its implementation.

It was difficult to find a focus for the redesign. The vision for Rank Xerox in 2000 and beyond provided a well-developed concept for how the organisation should work, providing models for culture behaviours and business process management, but this was difficult to translate to organisation and operational practices. The team examined ABB, Hewlett Packard, Texas Instruments and other obvious candidates but could not find a major theme relevant to Rank Xerox. Surprisingly enough, the answer came in the form of the technique first used by Rank Xerox in the 1980s – benchmarking. The extra factor in 1993 was the benchmarking of all business processes in all countries. With the help of a newly developed business process architecture, the performance of each process area was measured in all countries. The core process areas were:

☐ time to market (product development and launch)
☐ integrated supply chain (manufacturing and logistics)
☐ market to collection (marketing, sales and invoicing)
☐ customer service (after-sales service and support)
☐ finance, leasing and accounting
☐ infrastructure (quality, HRM, information management).

This analysis displayed wide variations in process performance from country to country. Although countries did not show such great variation in final results, the methods by which they achieved those results did vary widely. In some process areas the best and the worst performers varied by a factor of more than five. Another finding was that every country could point to at least some areas of excellence. It was not difficult to reach the conclusion that if every country achieved the level of the best practice for each process, the opportunity was very high, and that Rank Xerox could achieve the desired state across Europe by 1996. Significantly, that did not mean immediate total re-engineering; it required that each unit equal the best practice already achieved in Europe. This was still not an easy target, as working practices had developed over many years, were embedded in local cultures and systems and would require major effort to improve.

In Rank Xerox such analysis is very powerful – it is fact based, and visible. The annual quality self-assessment model could be used, where each unit is inspected by senior managers from other units, and best practices can be observed and shared. The team concluded that measurement at a high level was no longer enough. It was easy to see that general managers were responsible for the four corporate priorities. It was much more difficult to compare results for workgroups and functions from country to country, since the organisation and activities varied so widely. From a people perspective, it provided for the first time a set of comparable measures directly related to their areas of responsibility. It also provided for credible communication of the new organisation design and new performance goals. Although the message might be unwelcome, the basis for higher performance was not exhortation to work harder, but demonstration of an intelligent way to improve. Rank Xerox had to operate as a set of business processes, with measurements to track process performance at a much more detailed level, as this was the only way that the array of improvement actions could be managed.

The other major conclusion of the gap analysis was that quality and productivity go hand in hand with customer satisfaction and employee satisfaction. The analysis clearly showed that the smaller, simple units showed high performance in all the important factors. In the large countries many busy people were working for one another and not for the customer. The total assessed opportunity for Rank Xerox in Europe was 25 per cent productivity. These were not new numbers. All this information had been available for many years, but needed the awareness and insight provided by the 'crisis' of opportunity. It was a new way of analysing performance, which clearly demonstrated the opportunity to management and people throughout the company. The initial reactions to benchmarking usually include disbelief and rationalisation of the different levels of performance, and Rank Xerox is still no exception. Eventually, though, the general managers admitted that if the analysis was 50 per cent in error, that still left an unacceptable gap, and that the priority was to close the gap, not explain it away.

Gap analysis summary

- □ Productivity and quality go together.
- □ Small simple units have visibly higher performance.
- □ Large units have diseconomies of scale and higher complexity.
- □ Productivity improvements can be linked to key business processes.

Rank Xerox had to redirect energy into working for customers, generating growth and productivity. The gap analysis also helped to communicate to people. In Rank Xerox UK, employees who undoubtedly were working very hard, asked why the company was obsessed with cost reduction. The answer was that operating at 30 per cent below the European cost benchmark was not acceptable – but up till then, nobody had demonstrated that gap to the employees. The analysis served to communicate why re-engineering was necessary, why downsizing and redirection were necessary, and how growth could be achieved. The corporation had to articulate a rationale for growth, and why the inefficient practices embedded over many years of prior growth had to be removed before they became another crisis of failure.

Royal Bank of Scotland – preparing and moving forward

Leadership during a re-engineering programme is critical to its eventual success; it has to be visible and challenging, prepared to take risks and put itself at risk. The elements of visible and challenging leadership have been evident throughout the Royal Bank of Scotland's Columbus change programme. While chief executive Mathewson provided the broad framework and global vision for the Royal Bank, the Retail Bank managing director Tony Schofield had to craft and develop his own vision that would motivate and energise 14,000 people into action.

A key element in preparing the ground for change was the establishment of a Change Management Group (CMG) in early 1992. This was essentially the board of directors for the Retail Bank who were to meet every Thursday for the next three years to establish direction, review proposals and with whom every single element of the change programme was discussed. In the early days, every meeting was chaired by the chief executive. This in itself made it clear to everyone how serious the intent was to drive the change process.

Each of the core business processes, credit, service, personal sales, commercial and corporate business required detailed analysis to understand how the various processes functioned. To provide focus for this research, business initiative teams were established, led by a seasoned senior manager from the bank who was selected for his or her expertise in the particular area and, critically, their desire to make a contribution.

Each of the business initiative teams was staffed by a consultant who acted as personal coach to the team leader. In addition, they provided their considerable powers of analysis and intellect to challenge basic assumptions. Furthermore, the consultants also provided a channel for learning from other assignments to be introduced, examined and applied. To support the business initiative manager, a number of talented young managers were seconded from various areas of the bank. In addition, the Columbus programme director Cameron McPhail recruited young postgraduate students and first job-change graduates who had backgrounds in operations research, statistics and applied economics.

A potent learning laboratory was created with which parallels could be drawn to the 'skunk works' of General Electric. A genuine excitement pervaded everything the Columbus team members did. An identity was established complete with compass logo and very soon a powerful 'in-group' began to be established. The strength of belonging and ownership of the core processes would, in time, create its own problems as the 'Columbites' began to adopt the characteristics of 'Jedi knights' – a sense of certainty and absolute belief. In addition to the core process teams, other Columbus teams began to emerge. In particular, there were the 'solution space providers' of information technology, property and HR – the role of these teams was to provide solutions and resolve problems in their areas of responsibility.

For the first 15 months of the Columbus programme, the imperative was to gather data and analyse the root problems. However, as the change programme had been established on the basis that it would be self-funding, a number of 'quick wins' were identified whereby the bank could capitalise very early on from initial analysis, an example of this was the decision to reprice certain products.

Project director McPhail had recognised that the dictum of 'successful change programmes begin with results' was crucial to long-term success. Furthermore, before any business initiative project was sanctioned, it had to demonstrate a positive net present value, that proved conclusively the project's contribution over and above the bank investment criteria. Having crossed that hurdle, every single project and sub-project was scrutinised by the CMG at its weekly meetings. While to many the processes may sound bureaucratic, the range and scale of the problems confronting the teams were such that most solutions required board approval, particularly as the impact on key control measures, which in a bank are critical, could be profound.

The further into the change programme the bank went, the greater the realisation that while we were undertaking dramatic changes to all the core processes, the need to change was not going to go away – ever.

Toshiba – Preparing and moving forward

There was only one place to start; at the beginning. There was the potential to create an entirely new kind of organisation. The known quantity was the volume of television sets to be made at the start and there was a reasonable viewpoint on the potential for growth in at least the medium term. The mechanics of manufacturing were to be 'borrowed' from Toshiba Corporation in Japan and they were able to be translated into indicative numbers of workers directly involved with the manufacturing processes. Toshiba Japan was also able to offer a datum in respect of product quality standards. Product unit costs that were needed to be achieved in order for the operation to be viable could be identified. Longer-term viability would depend upon at least an efficient baseline in terms of cost and in terms of product quality. Essentially, viability was perceived to be dependent upon a capability to respond reliably to varying market needs; flexible processes and attitudes were therefore going to be of paramount importance.

Apart from the known and anticipated quantities, the 'how' of how to organise the operation was entirely open. What has become known as a 'blank page approach' was adopted by the team. The team decided that any and all options should be considered and, given that nothing could happen without the people involved in the enterprise, most of the focus of their activity should be on and around people issues, towards the achievement of quality (product and service) standards. Members were encouraged to express ideas and views forcibly, Geoffrey Deith indicated that common ground could be developed later. Deith made the starter-contribution himself, addressing 26 items, all of them personnel related. Always, the end view and standards were kept in mind – would what was being considered satisfy the base criteria? The range and detail of what was discussed, and the outcomes, are not outlined here but can be read in other published material.[38] Issues were addressed over a range of meetings, all of which took place during evenings, weekends and public holidays owing to the fact that those involved were mostly otherwise engaged in continuing to run the joint venture company. One of the team members estimated that during most of the planning processes, he was been able to 'enjoy' no more than about four hours sleep a night. In a concentrated two-month period, most of the framework had been outlined. Conceptually, all of the employees in the enterprise at whatever level would be involved in contributing to the operational objectives beyond the scope of individual job function. Participative processes would be put in place in sections, departments and at corporate level, at which there would be an entirely 'open book' approach with full disclosure of corporate information. Flexible staffing policies would have to be adopted which would have training development and remuneration implications. Teamworking in its widest sense would have to be taken into account including the special role and accountabilities of managers, first-line supervisors and individual team members. Open and visible communications processes would be vital.

It was soon realised that the keys to successful outcomes for all of these issues would be individual and collective attitudes. The selection of those to be employed in the new enterprise would need to be given special attention. A cascade approach was ultimately adopted whereby individuals, starting at the higher level, were selected by the top team, and thence involving lower management and supervision. There was however, to be no hierarchy, as effectively there were to be only three levels of management, and sometimes a senior manager was involved in selection at quite low level appointments, but with powers of veto and strong influence being exerted by the lowest level of management or supervision involved. Psychometric selection processes were not employed, decisions being arrived at through extensive interview processes (at least three, one by someone outside the area to be employed, to limit bias).

One of the most important parts of the selection processes was that of self-selection. Considerable measures were adopted to communicate to potential employees the standards and attitudes that would be demanded. Every employee was required, before pursuing an application, to read about the vision for the organisation and to watch a video produced especially for the purpose outlining the issues and the standards, and which gave a 'flavour' of the kind of organisation that was being aimed for. Individuals were invited to select themselves out if what they saw and heard was not in line with what they felt they would be comfortable with. The issue of selection, interestingly not an item on the original agenda, became one of the most important foundation processes for the new organisation.

In the recruitment video presented by Geoffrey Deith, five major characteristics were outlined that defined the qualities that would be required: expertise, enthusiasm, idealism, commitment and attention to detail. Deith gave an explanation of what was meant by each. The video went on to explain the standards required with regard to attendance, flexibility and workmanship. It indicated the extent to which the organisation would have to operate 'like clockwork' and set out the concepts for employment terms including single status conditions and involvement in the decisions of the company. A further video tape explained the workings of a proposed company advisory board (COAB) involving union and non-union representative employees at all levels. That video took the form of a discussion between Geoffrey Deith and Roy Sanderson, the EETPU National Officer, chaired by Graham Turner, a television journalist. Communications processes before, during and subsequent to the set-up were considered to be vital. Holistic design of all operational and support processes was also seen to be critical and no organisational concepts were accepted without wider consideration of the implications, and integration with people and operational systems. These included everything from conceptual job designs, reward packages, selection and training processes and how any difficulties that might be encountered would be resolved.

With the time-scales involved, it was not feasible to 'pilot' the new proposals. The best design the team could put together in wider consultation with others, including Union officials, had to be adopted. There would be no gentle run-in. The new organisation working to the standards which had been defined would have to work from Day One.

5

COPING WITH DISTRACTIONS

- ☐ The best counter-forces to distraction are consistent drive from the top and widespread awareness of early and ongoing success.
- ☐ Apathy is a significant negative force and must be positively addressed.
- ☐ Pace of roll-out affects distraction.
- ☐ Resistance has to be anticipated and minimised, outflanked or otherwise overcome. There are strategies that can be successfully adopted.
- ☐ Other projects can either undermine or support re-engineering. Careful co-ordination at least is required.

The greatest counter-forces to distractions and diversions are:

- ☐ strength of drive from the top
- ☐ awareness of success from the bottom.

The two, working together, provide the most powerful influence. Experience suggests that either of them in the absence of the other will be competing against negative forces. Apathy is probably the most common negative force. Apathy is not neutral; like the saying goes, 'If you're not for us, then you're against us'.

Positive criticism

That is not to say that forces critical of BPR actions are always necessarily negative. It is the timing and extent of involvement to take into account those critical comments that matters. If they are taken aboard early enough they will probably help forge a more satisfactory outcome. In Toshiba's case, the managing director, who was also the project director, encouraged expression of the most extreme or contrary viewpoints, seeking afterwards, through discussion and analysis, to find the common ground that would take into account the most appropriate and universally acceptable solution. It is to be acknowledged that not many people in a large organisation have the opportunity to express contrary views at the planning stage. The ideal is to take into account the widest inputs at all levels, as exemplified by the case of The Leicester Royal Infirmary, which was pursuing change not from the trigger of a crisis but from a challenge to achieve massive improvements in patient care, teaching and research. The circumstances will to an extent determine the span of involvement. Where, in Toshiba's case, the final re-engineered design had to be completed within about two months, scope for widest involvement was distinctly limited; the key here for getting things right was the quality of the operational and functional representation and those individuals' attitude, including, in this case, significant positive input by a national officer of a Union on behalf of and in the interests of employees involved rather than at that time in any formal representational capacity.

Involvement has two dimensions; first, scope to receive constructive comment (constructively creative or constructively critical). Criticism is not necessarily destructive. It would hardly be destructive, for example, for a construction worker involved in a new building to indicate that a design was such, in his experience, to render the process of construction unsafe. In that case, construction engineering science may have the solution to avoid the problem, if but only if the correct method and specifications are adhered to all the way through. One of the authors, early in his career, was being conducted round a factory of a major electrical appliance manufacturer by the works director. Every question that he put to the works director the director redirected! He consistently passed every question to the nearest manufacturing operative involved, indicating that they (the operatives) 'probably knew more about the process than anyone in management'. The director had in fact been employed in that factory all his working life, having started as a craft apprentice, yet he acknowledged the wisdom and worth of the humblest worker ... and they loved him for it.

These points are being made not just in support of the value of contribution from the lowest level but that such involvement can contribute significantly, at the right stage, to avoidance of distractions and diversions by having more likely got things right.

Too much of a good thing

Too much involvement of the wrong kind and at the wrong stage can be as bad as none at all. Procrastination and analysing things to death may do a lot for democracy but won't do much for organisational efficiency, certainly in the time-scales probably required. 'Just do it', is the recommendation of one top executive. One 80 per cent right decision, carried through with conviction may more likely succeed than a carefully orchestrated and carefully conducted consultative process. A road bypass scheme near one of the author's homes has, with great care, been under discussion for some 10 years. Millions have been spent and, if final agreement on a route is achieved within two years (which is by no means certain), the new road may be in place three years beyond that. Where changes are required to be being delivered within 15 months rather than 15 years, compromises on consensus may have to be accepted. Getting the best model/design is more likely to be achieved with a small but representative team of the best brains and knowledge available, testing that out under 'laboratory' conditions if possible to verify the viability, then getting on with it ... *Just do it!*

Counter-resistance planning

Assuming the very best design, there will nevertheless be resistance to be coped with. A counter-resistance plan must be made. Options include:

□ minimising the resistance
□ outflanking the resistance
□ confronting and overpowering the resistance.

These issues, in general terms, are dealt with in Chapter 4,

'Preparing and Moving Forward', but need here to be considered in operational context.

Toshiba, to an extent, outflanked and minimised resistance by creating a condition whereby everything *had* to start from scratch. Maintenance of the *status quo* was negated literally by closing down the plant, paying off everybody and re-hiring under a new legal and psychological contract. Bass had its resistance minimised by the Government, which determined that Bass had fundamentally to restructure through 'losing' some 40 per cent of their public house outlets. The Leicester Royal Infirmary minimised resistance through direct involvement of the staff involved and by undertaking extensive communications of both formal and pseudo-informal kinds ... literally, talking to everyone.

Power and perceptions

It can be said that resistance to change is proportional to the impact upon the culture and the shifting power introduced by the change. Thus, when a changing culture is accompanied by a shifting power, resistance is compounded. Ansoff asserts, but here we refute, that resistance will be inversely proportional to the length of time over which the change is spread.[39] This is anathema to re-engineering, where the first-move advantage coupled with speedy implementation forges change. The greater the clarity and forcefulness in the implementation, the more likely is success. Avoiding being distracted requires great clarity and purpose of mind. There is a tendency from people to conclude, particularly if the announcements lack clarity, that the impending changes are not necessary or not relevant. Even if change seems partially relevant, there will be a tendency by affected individuals and groups to exaggerate the negative impacts. Further, without clarity and reinforcement there will be a tendency, either by those who will benefit, perhaps, from the change or those who will not be affected, to assume that they will be affected and that they will suffer. Perceptions will be that the positive outcomes of the change have been deliberately exaggerated. These reactions will be hardly surprising within those organisations that have been subject to discontinuous changes in the past, changes that have patently not worked and have been discarded or merely faded away.

Clarity of purpose

The true need and the impact of not responding to the imperatives that are bringing about the requirements for change must be made clear and unequivocal, particularly if the cause is external to the organisation (as with Bass). Where the driver is internal to the organisation, as with The Leicester Royal Infirmary, where the need for change is as a result of a challenge to find a better way, then greater reliance will have to be put on converting positive support for the change through 'proving' both the results and the process in pilot projects, in which a wide range of staff are involved. Converting resistance to positive support is extremely difficult but can be achieved when the perception of the crisis or opportunity is sufficiently clear, and especially when there is a charismatic leader to rally round.

Overcome covert resistance

Under most circumstances, even when resistance has been reduced, there will still be individuals who mount overt or covert resistance. This resistance must be overcome and the 'power card' might have to be used and individuals 'removed' (sacked, dismissed, made redundant, retired or transferred). This is not extolling immoral action, but merely recognising that for the wider good resistance has to be removed if all the alternative strategies have not otherwise modified it. It would, in our view, be immoral to rely upon removal as the only counter-resistance tactic. It would also be bad business.

Planning and other projects

A clear implementation plan is vital to minimise distractions and diversions, for both implementation of the planning and implementation of the plan. Distractions, diversions and resistance must be anticipated. Contingency plans, in terms of budget, etc., must be made. Projects that are planned to, or may run parallel, have to be evaluated in terms of the extent to which they support or underpin BPR initiatives, detract from them in terms of time, attention or resources, or even run contrary to BPR actions.

The planners, in looking at these issues, may develop a clear understanding of how everything might link together, but it will be necessary selectively to convey the broader picture to the wider team. Too much detail, nevertheless, may serve to confuse and itself distract. The balance between openness on the one hand and relevance on the other may be a fine one and only those involved can make judgements as to what the best balance might be. Time to consider these issues, and the time and investment needed for effective communication, must be taken into account.

Bass Taverns had two significant projects to tie in. The first was the introduction of a new computer-based information and communications system that has been in the planning before the BPR initiatives but which became a fundamental building block for some of the changes that were to take place in management and operational processes. Bass also, concurrent with the BPR initiatives, launched a total quality programme that, again, interfaced with and underpinned re-engineering initiatives. Rank Xerox, while accepting step-change, had ongoing total quality management (TQM) programmes aimed at significant but smaller step-change.

TQM and BPR are not one and the same thing. They certainly share many of the same features but they require different handling. It is rather like comparing a marathon run with a hundred metre sprint and saying they are both the same, ie running. They require quite different kinds of preparation and different strengths. TQM and BPR are both about delivering change but it is probably in the scale and pace of change that they differ most. If they are to work effectively together, their key interfaces and programming must be co-ordinated.

Project mutuality
Professor Eric Lawler, undertaking research in the USA into the effectiveness of TQM initiatives, has, for example, been able to indicate that TQM on its own, while adding value, perhaps significantly so, is considerably enhanced by employee involvement programmes. When dealt with as individual and uncoordinated initiatives, the results are not as favourable as when dealt with as a combined initiative. The value gained is,

as it were, *more* than the sum of their parts. Nevertheless, if such issues do not seem relevant to each other to those involved – say, management on the one hand involving employees in a very open and participative way and, on the other, effecting other change by top-down direction – there will be mixed messages. The outcome, in those circumstances, has the potential to be *less* than the sum of their parts. Appropriateness of initiatives, and the way those initiatives will work together, is a matter for conscious review and co-ordination of planning and action.

Maintaining impetus

To avoid distractions, diversions and resistance, taking and maintaining the initiative after careful planning, and then maintaining the impetus, will greatly reduce the scope for distractions to be sustained. If the subsequent intervention causes a change in direction or halt to procedures, that would be an indication that contingency planning had been inadequate. Employee involvement will contribute more at the planning stage but communications need to be extensively followed through at the implementation stage.

Coping with casualties

In most major change processes there will be casualties of a terminal kind and many walking wounded. How the survivors perceive the treatment of the casualties will condition the extent to which they present distractions or resistance. It cannot be assumed that because someone is not disadvantaged or is even benefitting directly from the change, that they will not be adversely affected. The impact upon them of the effects upon others should not be under estimated. Their emotions can range from anger on the one hand, because of perceived 'unfair' treatment of others, to grief and even guilt relating to the fact that they have 'survived', and others haven't. The syndrome, 'survivor syndrome', is well recognised in connection with great natural disasters, and those affected need help and support.

Supporting survivors

Counselling for casualties will not be enough; equivalent support mechanisms will need to be provided for the benefit of 'survivors'. Again, this must be anticipated and provided for. The nature of the support required will depend upon the extent of the impact of the change, and who is involved. It should not be assumed that a 'sympathetic ear' will be sufficient. Professional support will be required to provide direct counselling as well as coaching of line or other managers within the organisation, to enable them to provide some support and know the limitations of what they can do.

Dealing with other distractions

External 'interference' or impact that could not have been reasonably foreseen, such as a new government policy, a judicial ruling or a change in ownership of the organisation, can all substantially impact upon the change programme. Dealing openly and visibly with the issue, quickly and efficiently, is probably the only universal response that is appropriate. The nature of the response will depend upon the issue, but the manner of involvement and actions needs to be compatible with the planned and ongoing initiatives if pursuit of the original objective is to be maintained and sustained.

Bass Taverns – coping with distractions and diversions

The distractions and diversion pressures that Bass experienced were, broadly:

(a) External interference or threats. To some degree the Bass Taverns change programme was launched to cope with the threat of the imposition of the Office of Fair Trading/Department of Trade and Industry regulations and only recently we have had to comply with another request for information as a result of a new Office of Fair Trading investigation into the price of beer for our lessees in comparison with our free trade customers. We are better able to cope with this and other external 'interferences' as a result of our change programme experiences than we have been in the past.

(b) Internal interference, eg the 'time card'. We found that this
     was the ultimate delaying tactic of management opposed
     to change and new ways of working. With us, it went
     something like this ... 'We are of course with you all the
     way, but given that it is now just coming up to Christmas
     and a peak trading time in the pubs, why don't we agree to
     put off the implementation of the project until the spring
     of next year.' It is usually followed by 'Well, of course, we
     are now up to our eyeballs in budgets, let us start in the
     early summer', which is followed by 'In the last instance
     we will definitely do it when we have the peak summer
     trade behind us'. The lonely world of the last instance
     never comes!

We coped with such responses in the following ways: (a) Picked
the opponents off one by one, not letting them meet under BPR
auspices. (b) Used the 'first move' advantage, such as 'Why
don't you give it a go then the benefits in terms of profits will
quickly accrue to your patch', sometimes coupled with 'It will
be crystal clear to the board who is really behind the change
programme'. We found that with one on board, the rest tended
to follow. The herding instinct among senior executives is
probably as powerful in Bass as it is in most organisations.

We demonstrated success though a successful pilot. The
pilot executive, in pioneer mode, has got too much to lose to
make the pilot anything but a huge success story. We made
sure that the chief executive officer visited the pilot and we
made sure that the whole world knew the story.

Total compliance and total involvement of all of our people
was essential. We got all kinds of serendipity effects – unin-
tended consequences and benefits; we had to keep our eyes
open for them. This brings in another role for HR professionals. We had to watch and listen throughout the pilot
programmes and the start of implementation to identify best
practice and then share it.

Sometimes we faced functional resistance. In response to a
comment such as 'We can't do that', the offer or threat of bringing in consultants 'to do it' usually did the trick.

We were managing, against conventional wisdom, a variety
of change and quality improvement programmes. These maintained compatibility and avoided conflict through considerable

attention to communications and co-ordination. The last thing we wanted was the equivalent of the Gas Board digging the hole in the road and filling it in just before the Electricity Board needed a hole in the same place!

The Leicester Royal Infirmary – coping with distractions

The external context

The reform of the National Health Service since the early 1990s has given a significant degree of autonomy to organisations such as The Leicester Royal Infirmary. In fact, without NHS Trust status, the hospital would not have been able to embark on such a radical change programme. However, The Leicester Royal Infirmary operates within a national system. In that respect it is a comparatively small organisation. This has some major implications for the re-engineering programme:

(a) The boundaries and salary scales of professional jobs are nationally agreed and have grown up over the last 40 years. The type of job roles developed through the re-engineering programme intrinsically challenge this. The process of managing this involves discussions with national professional bodies. It has to be sensitively handled and can take a long time. The implementation of local pay determination is in its early days.

(b) The nationally determined indicators by which the performance of an NHS Trust is measured are sometimes at odds with a re-engineered organisation. An example of this is the 'efficiency index' by which the efficiency of every NHS hospital is measured. The Leicester Royal Infirmary has transformed its outpatient services so that many patients have to visit the hospital on only one occasion to have tests carried out, a medical consultation and results. Previously this would have required three or four visits to the hospital. However, by seeing each patient only once, the hospital gets a lower performance score on the efficiency index than by seeing them on several occasions.

Through its re-engineering programme, The Leicester Royal Infirmary is challenging much of the national *status quo*. It makes the re-engineering effort doubly difficult – the external environment and its framework has been re-invented as well as the internal environment. The performance measurement framework reflects the aims and core values of the re-engineering programme. Targets are categorised as follows, and are quantified using either direct or proxy measures:

☐ Achieving world-class clinical outcomes from healthcare processes.
☐ Optimising patient, purchaser and staff satisfaction.
☐ Improving teaching and research opportunities.
☐ Valuing time.
☐ Ensuring that the time invested in healthcare is to the maximum benefit of the patient by reducing delays and unnecessary work.
☐ Valuing resources.
☐ Improving the efficiency of the use of each human, physical and financial resource in the hospital to ensure value for money.

The measures also reflect the strategic priorities of The Leicester Royal Infirmary. When the re-engineering programme is completed, the measurement structure will provide a framework for sustaining and continuously improving the gains made.

Internal inference

Experience from The Leicester Royal Infirmary re-engineering programme has identified the following mechanisms which have been used successfully to deal with internal inference:

☐ Ensure that the organisational leadership is providing the best possible role model in terms of its own priorities and actions.
☐ Ensure that re-engineering is the only quality improvement activity in the organisation. If other initiatives are important they should be incorporated within the re-engineering programme. Otherwise they should stop.
☐ Build re-engineering targets into the key objective of every manager and clinical team.
☐ Make sure that senior managers guide and support middle managers in their prioritisation process.

☐ Don't waste too much time and energy, particularly at the early stages, on trying to win over cynics to the programme. Concentrate on supporting the innovators who want to lead the change process. Demonstrating results is the best way to win over the majority of people to new ways of working. After this has happened peer pressure will bring over most sceptics.

☐ Stick to the moral high ground. Link the re-engineering programme to the strategic direction and the vision of the hospital of the future. Re-engineering is only a mechanism for achieving this.

☐ Communicate genuine success widely.

☐ Build in the organisational learning from the programme. When things don't go to plan, evaluate what went wrong with key stakeholders and action plan how to build these lessons into the programme.

☐ Evaluate success as well as failure.

☐ Build in time to reflect with key stakeholders.

☐ Keep communicating in a targeted appropriate way and keep listening.

Impact on other change programmes

As stated previously, the organisation decided to take a fairly ruthless approach with other quality improvement programmes while running the re-engineering programme. A particular syndrome to avoid is that of 'tidying up the room while the bulldozer waits outside'. In an organisation the size of The Leicester Royal Infirmary, there are many change initiatives going on and it is difficult to keep track of them. An important step forward at The Leicester Royal Infirmary was to 'vision' the role of quality in a post-re-engineered hospital. This was compared with the quality function of the hospital today and used to build a transition strategy for the future. It led to an important alignment between the re-engineering programme and the quality programme within the hospital. Quality facilitators will play a key role in the hospital of the future. The re-engineered solutions will require ongoing measurement, feedback and development, through an incremental approach. Preparation for this role has commenced.

Rank Xerox – coping with distractions

For Rank Xerox the main distraction throughout the implementation was managing the day-to-day business to achieve the results already committed for 1993–94. At one point Fournier was heard to observe, after another long implementation review, 'Well, I just hope somebody out there is managing this business while we redesign it.' In fact, the 1993 results continued the stable trend of the previous years, perhaps showing that the company was running on momentum rather than any management intervention capable of accelerating performance. It was precisely this inertia that Fournier was determined to break. There was initial scepticism, but surprisingly little resistance among senior managers once the approach had been agreed, despite the radical change to the nature of a general manager's job. Probably the main factors in achieving this were:

- [ ] the vision of 'Rank Xerox 2000' already in place, which laid the ground for real culture change
- [ ] the solid background of quality management
- [ ] the participative nature of the design, with frequent reviews at board level
- [ ] the conclusive results of the process and productivity analysis
- [ ] allowing the new entities to implement at their own pace
- [ ] not least, the early success of the new organisation in growing revenue and reducing costs in 1994.

Royal Bank of Scotland – coping with distractions

The swiftness of CEO Mathewson's moves gave first advantage to the change agents. However, radical and sustained change can and will only be realised in a climate where everyone can identify with a super-ordinate goal. In the case of the Royal Bank of Scotland, the goal was to return to profitability, enhance shareholder and customer value and retain independence. However, relatively few except those close to the top recognised that maintaining the *status quo* was not an option, the bank had to change.

The role of communicating the vision and, importantly, how the vision is to be realised is arguably one of the keys to successful change. At group level, Mathewson began with an annual results video, highlighting the business performance and most important of all, putting himself on the spot, answering questions of which he had no prior knowledge, direct from members of staff. This represented a sea-change for staff in the bank who had previously seen little of the leadership let alone been able to ask audacious questions without fear of reprisal. What Mathewson did was lead by example, believing that if a leader wants to create 'followship', they have to first of all establish their credentials and convince people they are worth following.

The Retail Bank managing director Tony Schofield, together with his co-directors and in particular the director of Columbus, McPhail, worked extremely hard at establishing their own parallel communications programme, designed to explain and educate. A key element of the communications process was to establish the notion of super-ordinate goal. This is not and has never been an easy task. Although the Hong Kong and Shanghai Bank had made a hostile takeover bid in the 1980s, which was rebutted on referral to the Monopolies and Mergers Commission, most staff in the bank had little real insight into the wholesale changes taking place in the financial services sector.

Life was quite comfortable; in return for dogged execution of tasks and, for those in managerial roles, frequent job moves and a career profile as a generalist banker, they were rewarded adequately and held positions of status in the community.

The twin pressures of mounting bad debts and increased competition began to bite into previously cherished security. Schofield, in particular, after a lifetime in banking could make a plausible case for change that would address the scepticism of the middle managers. He had to work extremely hard spending up to 50 per cent of his time on the road meeting staff at all levels, listening to their fears and communicating his vision for a better tomorrow. The communication process was designed to touch as many people as possible at all levels – an unprecedented step – and importantly it created a bridge from the top of the hierarchy to the bottom in one move. In doing so, Schofield engaged all staff in meaningful dialogue but, importantly realising it was the managers who were most under threat, he made sure his message remained undiluted among the most junior staff.

Over time the messages became institutionalised via video and regular 'cascade' briefings. These were designed to announce milestones and critical steps in the change programme. During 1994 three separate communications cascades were held to announce substantial human resource changes. The process designed to reach all 14,500 staff over a two-week period began with up to 500 selected managers being trained and briefed on the content and concepts. Furthermore, all briefing managers were measured on the impact and comprehension of the message by their staff, via reviews and feedback questionnaires. To secure further the attention of managers, all were given a Key Result Area (KRA) – a measure of performance, directly related to the quality, content and delivery of the communication cascade.

Having an excellent process of communication is one thing, having something to communicate is another. Very early on it was recognised that the Retail board would only communicate when it had something to say. Furthermore, it was also recognised that how the message was being communicated was equally important as the content. As a consequence, mixed media have always been used, including video, focus groups, briefings and magazines.

The core process redesign model presented a template for the communication process as it gave a rationale for all decisions being taken (Figure 5.1).

All business initiative teams adopted this model and regularly introduced competitive data in the planning and scoping phase. In doing so this exposed even greater numbers of staff to our position relative to our competitors and other comparators. During the design and development phase, the initiative teams also consulted widely across the bank, in doing so increasing the change constituency and reinforcing the super-ordinate goal – to embrace change and increase the chances that the vision could be realised. Testing of pilot schemes led by the Columbus business initiative teams allowed considerable learning to take place, which together with a phased release of the roll-out ensured valuable lessons learned could be acted upon swiftly.

The planned approach to change minimised the potential for organisational indigestion and by embracing an ever increasing number of 'part-time change consultants' among the staff, widened the change franchise and minimised disruption, road blocks and major errors in implementation.

Figure 5.1

ROYAL BANK OF SCOTLAND'S PROCESS REDESIGN MODEL

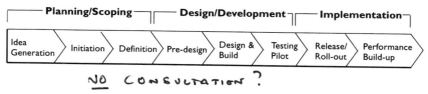

The key to minimising distractions and diversions was the whole-hearted participation of the top team demonstrated by their willingness to commit both time and resources. In addition, clarity of vision, communicating that vision and widening the change franchise, ensured 'transplant' or 'tissue rejection' was kept to a minimum.

Toshiba – coping with distractions

Once things were set in train there were few distractions and diversions but this was not by chance. Major potential diversions had been foreseen:

☐ trade union interference from 'unsympathetic' or 'unrepresentative' unions
☐ constraints of the existing employee contracts
☐ 'old style' attitudes, especially among managerial and supervisory staff.

Strategies were developed to deal with all of these. The key strategy was to provide a clear playing field, if at all possible, for entirely new terms and conditions of employment. This was not a time when the market-place and the industrial relations climate nationally was conducive to such initiatives. But even if the costs were to be high, it was felt that a way had to be found. The way that was found was both dramatic and expensive, and was certainly not straightforwardly in the interests of Toshiba's joint venture partner or the unions involved, of which there were seven. The solution was on the margins of what was legally possible at that time and which in Britain would not be legally possible now. The action was to make *everyone* in the joint venture redundant, providing an equitable termination package and then selecting and engaging, for what was to be an entirely new company, employees on entirely new terms and conditions of employment.

Rank was less than enthusiastic about the proposal; they held 70 per cent of the shares of the joint venture company and stood to bear 70 per cent of the redundancy costs and costs relating to job generation and outplacement. Given that less than 20 per cent of the employees in the joint venture were likely to secure employment in the new company, they were unlikely to favour this course of action. Ultimately, however, agreement was reached for the joint venture to close totally and for the partners to bear the costs relative to the proportions of their share holdings.

The strategy containing these actions was determined well in advance of any public announcement or consultations with employees and was a fundamental element of the termination agreement between Rank and Toshiba. Its achievement by Toshiba gave them the level playing field opportunity they had been looking for. Had it not been achieved, it is more than possible that Toshiba would have walked away and, despite adverse short-term business implications, have set up on a greenfield site somewhere else.

To avoid unhelpful union interference and unrepresentative representation was by no means straightforward. The choice was:

(a) to recognise no unions at all and set up a non-union shop
(b) to allow representative unions to apply for recognition, subsequent to set-up
(c) to hold a 'beauty parade' of interested unions and 'select' the union or unions that seemed most appropriate
(d) to select a single union to represent the interests of all employees.

For the avoidance of union demarcation difficulties, options (a), (d) and possibly (c) seemed to Toshiba to be the only viable ones. Option (a), the non-union approach was attractive and, given that the plant was not in a particularly strong union-oriented area, was considered viable. The opportunity would be open nevertheless in the future for different unions to aspire to represent different groups of employees, recruiting members in competition with other unions. This could, in the long term, be divisive to Toshiba's interests. However, constructive approaches from the EETPU seeking to represent the interests of all employees put paid to all other considerations and ultimately led to the notable single-union deal. It was not, however, the 'carve-up' that has been portrayed by some.

The EETPU represented the vast majority of employees in the joint venture company. It was unquestionably an appropriate union to the industry in which Toshiba would be engaged. The trigger that prompted Toshiba to select the EETPU was the thoroughness with which they had investigated the needs and attitudes of Japanese industrialists and they genuinely appeared to be seeking a new way for the avoidance of industrial conflict. Indeed, on a 'blank page' basis their stated aims and objectives for their members were not so different from the aims and objectives that were likely to be sought by Toshiba for its employees. A partnership was conceived and came into formal being with the signing of a sole representation agreement for the EETPU to represent all graded employees.

The opportunity, through restarting the entity, enabling the company to set entirely new terms and conditions led to being able to do the single-union deal with the EETPU. With creative input from the Union, discussions led to novel communications processes and novel provisions for the resolution of any difficulties that arose, which became characterised as 'pendulum arbitration'.

The conceptualisation of a company advisory board with representatives of union and non-union employees from all levels within the organisation was of particular importance. It was possible to indicate that while short-term decisions would have to be taken unilaterally by a management, these would be taken responsibly and would be open to review through the processes that would be set up. Short-term opposition to any initiative was thereby at least deferred until the establishment of the 'new' enterprise. The main perceived difficulties would be demotivation from among those who aspired to join the new enterprise but who would not for one reason or another be selected, conflicting with the interests of those who would be joining the new enterprise but who would have ongoing responsibilities in the joint venture until that closed.

The gap between the closure of the joint venture and the new company was perceived to be only two or three weeks at most. In one sense, although time was against the new company interests with little time to plan and set up something new, the time limit worked well for the new enterprise in that everything was happening so fast and in such a resolute way that concerted action by any individual or group against the initiatives was extremely difficult. Nevertheless, engendering a 'new spirit' in an increasingly depressing surroundings of a plant that was about to 'close' was not entirely easy. Most of the final induction and training could only take place in a small window before start-up. There was nevertheless a clear statement of what was going to be expected in the new enterprise and that everything to do with the new standards, methods and attitudes required in the new enterprise would come into play on Day One of its opening.

Gentle change was not considered, as old, inappropriate, attitudes might prevail. The new company had to start as it meant to go on and the term 'shock treatment' was coined as a target change model. At every stage the company aimed for and achieved control. The exercise was not about consultation and communication, it was about top-down action aimed towards egalitarian outcomes. It was a management-led revolution but towards a model that was both open and fair and which would be open to review when more participative practices could be put in place.

6

FUNDAMENTAL CHANGE FOR MANAGERS AND MANAGEMENT

- ☐ Fundamental change for managers and management is inevitable.
- ☐ Help is required for most managers to make the transition. With support and training, most managers can succeed.
- ☐ Not handling required changes in management will ensure lack of success.
- ☐ Leadership qualities are needed more than ever, but they are different in kind.
- ☐ Effective managers will gain rather than lose power.

In an organisation undergoing business process re-engineering, there are no processes so consistently affected as the processes of management. With BPR, there will always need to be fundamental change for managers and management; this brings immediate problems. Managers have more invested in the *status quo* than any other group. They have gained their status and their power through acquisition and exercise of particular skills and behaviours under an existing regime. Their arena of operations has often been subject to a 'game', where political adroitness and the exercise of command through power has been the order of things. They have been the controllers and the disseminators of information. They have used information for 'trading' purposes, perhaps within a power matrix and with struggles for political control between functions. They have been the ones to accept (or not) analyses, decide outcomes and direct others in the execution. Life, for the successful, has been rewarding, both for the ego and the pocket.

Vanishing boundaries

In a new order of things where the delineation of functional boundaries will vanish or diminish, where information, through technology and other forms of open access and sharing, will become common property, where individuals and groups not hitherto involved in participating in analysis and decision making become empowered to act without prior reference to anyone resembling what has previously been accepted as someone in a supervisory role, managers will consider they will be losing out. Real or imagined anticipation that their roles will become redundant will do nothing for self-confidence at management, as at other levels; when fighting for life the animal instinct is to fight back. It is hardly surprising therefore that inadequate attention to management processes and the changing roles of managers will render BPR open to resistance of both overt and covert kinds; the latter being especially undermining.

Managing middle managers

The roles of lower level middle managers will be especially affected by BPR activity but those higher in an organisation may have much to lose and will probably be well placed to launch effective counter offensives or delaying tactics. Without great awareness of the issues and the design and delivery of countervailing solutions, together with relentless and sometimes ruthless pressure from the top, managers will smother a re-engineering initiative.

When acting in contrary or unhelpful ways, managers may not be consciously malevolent or even deliberately resisting change. They may be merely acting in conformity with their experience and training to date. Managing manager resistance is not only what is required; engaging positive contributions and developing new ways of managing acceptable to those who have other requisite skills and knowledge is what is needed. 'Letting-go' in favour of something new can be a wholly satisfying experience, but thinking about it beforehand can be harrowing. The harrowing times have to be supported.

New ways have to be found, appropriate to new needs of the organisation and designed specifically for them. These will not generally be found outside, from text-book models or through recruiting particular skills and knowledge. The required changes both to organisational and job-role structures and to individual and collective behaviours will have to be made from within the organisation at every level and across the organisation.

Compatibility and communal effort

New management processes and systems will need to be compatible across the organisation but not necessarily uniform, and all involved will need to support those systems. That means that everyone, not just 'managers', will need to be involved. It will be no use empowering non-management individuals and groups to take up new accountabilities if they are unprepared or are unwilling. On the basis of what might be called support vectors, *every* individual operating against the effort required to move in a given direction will negate the effort of someone operating in support of the 'right' direction. Every individual operating in a different direction will pull the organisation off its intended course, according to the direction pulled and the amount of power applied. The need in BPR is to get *all* of the people pulling together in the same and required direction. For this, there needs to be mutuality between vision, goals and effort, not just for some individuals but for all individuals. The direction and power of pull have a combined effect; the more senior the person, the more power they will have available to influence. Managers have more power the higher up the structure they are, and in this context they warrant particular attention.

Team interfaces

One aspect of management that has to be commented upon is the need for a complete alignment in the balance of different levels and roles of management. For every complete team (relating, say, to a complete process), the interrelationship between them and the management team immediately superior, and the team(s) alongside accountable for other complete processes – the connecting links and interventions each way must be in balance. In an extreme but not untypical example, if the management of one complete process has significantly changed through, say, empowerment and change of systems, the benefits of that re-engineering will be undermined if the top management in that enterprise continue to act autocratically, not understanding what is going on down below. Every member of the top team 'sponsoring' one or more aspects of re-engineering (as with Bass) can help build bridges of understanding. The difficulties can be replicated laterally. To that extent, re-engineering may not be complete until the whole management system has been re-engineered. This will probably lead to wider structural change. (For a useful model of organisational system viability, see Stafford Beer.)[40]

Structural outcomes

There is no *one* way that re-engineered organisations are structured. There are, however, some outcomes that are common to many organisations:

☐ flatter organisations with less hierarchy and bureaucracy
☐ more teamwork and cross-organisational co-operation
☐ operations built around processes rather than functions
☐ hands-off management rather than hands-on management.

The one thing that does not go away, but possibly changes in kind, is the need for good leadership.

Confidence and change capability

A problem at the outset of BPR is that, before commencing the process, managers will not know what their new roles will be like after re-engineering. To face such a challenge confidently takes a degree of bravery on the part of the individuals concerned. That 'bravery', like in a military engagement, needs to be prepared for; a considerable amount of support from their organisation and top managers is certainly required. If individuals can be successfully conditioned to feel confident about changed roles and who then want to change, their chances of changing are really quite good. Some will find it totally impossible; some will relish the opportunities and find the process relatively easy; but the vast majority will only succeed if they are prepared for the process of change and the emergence of new roles. To feel confident about changed roles, individuals will need to understand that:

□ the organisation recognises their difficulties and will allow them leeway to make errors, but not to keep on making the same errors

□ to avoid making errors, training in new skills and sensitivities is required and will be provided

□ leadership skills and abilities are needed in greater measure than before but the emphasis will be different

□ there may be casualties but, if there are, what those casualties can expect in the way of support and succour

□ what the vision is for the exercise of managerial responsibilities under the likely new structure.

More, but different power

Rather than lose power, managers, by whatever name they are called at different levels within re-engineered organisations, will, if operating effectively, more usually gain power. It will be power that will need to be earned, rather than reflected from the status of the job. That power will most likely significantly come from the exercise of influence external to what will probably be a more empowered team and, on their behalf, representing their needs within the wider organisation, gaining appropriate resources, making linkages for cross-functional and cross-process co-operation and removing barriers. Internal challenges and emphasis are likely to be concentrated upon developing and coaching individuals and the team to reach their optimum potential. The exercise of power through giving directions will be substituted by a requirement to provide direction.

Earned power, compared with reflected power, is easier for an individual to live up to. It is less absolute. It more readily admits the affirmation of humanity. Individuals can acknowledge that others may have greater knowledge or skill. Far from looking weaker, those who are prepared to seek help from others gain in perceived stature and respect. In such a climate, individuals are more likely to readily acknowledge shortcomings in themselves and be conditioned to more readily address them, particularly when help is offered from someone who they respect.

Managers as coaches and facilitators

Coaching activities are one of the most common forms of skill needed to be developed in re-engineered organisations. Those in leadership roles will need them in good measure. To facilitate effective change at any level, and to manage the continuum, managers will need coaching and process skills beyond anything hitherto required. Engaging the involvement and effective contribution of individuals and teams in designing and implementing entirely new ways of doing things is critical to success. Success is more likely to be achieved when the skills, knowledge and abilities of the wider team are harnessed for the common good. Effective facilitation demands particular sensitivities and skills, including:

- [ ] being able to see, and convey, the bigger picture
- [ ] knowing how to involve people productively in issue identification and analysis
- [ ] capability to listen attentively and reflectively
- [ ] clarity of face-to-face and written communication
- [ ] capability to challenge and envision for improved ways of doing things and to engender confidence to be different or propose 'risky' actions.

Changes of role emphasis

Classic managerial responsibilities will have a continuum but may be exercised in different ways and with different emphases ...

- [ ] managing performance and expectations (less assessing; more involvement)
- [ ] building an environment where learning is encouraged and supported (less telling)

- ☐ coaching directly and ensuring coaching by others, according to the skills required (more hands-on activity for the manager; more monitoring of capabilities)
- ☐ resolving differences and conflict (less exercise of power; more rational/consensus agreement)
- ☐ engendering team unity and effort (more social emphasis)
- ☐ keeping everyone's eyes on the required goals (more visibility of goals and openness of performance achievements)
- ☐ ensuring the balance of abilities and skills are available and utilised (greater skills and more involvement within and outside the team regarding resourcing decisions)
- ☐ engendering trust and openness (more open admission of shortcomings and more practising what is preached; more consistency)
- ☐ integrating the efforts and involvement of others outside the particular sphere of responsibility (elimination of, rather than less, functional competition)
- ☐ managing processes need monitoring activities and managing in different ways than functions (more attention to information management, both technological and people-related)
- ☐ exercising persistence (more effort combined with more tact)

Consideration at all stages

All the issues covered in this chapter need to be considered by the BPR project team, both in the design and before the implementation phases of BPR. Resources (human and monetary), to address the arising needs, will be required in considerable measure. Without adequately addressing the needs relating to managers and management, re-engineering of business processes will not be undertaken successfully.

Bass Taverns – fundamental change for managers and management

The changes at Bass were fundamental. We were not in the world of fooling ourselves or organisational tinkering, nor were we in a world of just modifying a process. The Bass Taverns case is about radical transformation. It embraced an holistic approach. Not only did we address the issue of our core processes and our strategic direction but we also re-organised the company along process lines. We, therefore, attained our goals in terms of a fundamental shift in the curve of performance. In the same way we avoided the all too often organisational 'immune response' which happens in BPR failures when processes are changed without addressing the need to win the hearts and minds of all involved, as well as changing the structures to align with the new processes.

Managing a process-oriented organisation was, in Bass Taverns' case, about setting the people free, and the most important source of that freedom and empowerment was information. We adopted the analogy from Plato, where information or knowledge was an important source of power. All too often, in the context of our industry, information was used as such, eg the stocktaker with his special knowledge and skill descending on the pub manager to 'do his stock' and find out 'what was going on in the business' or the young area manager arriving with the pub profit and loss account and saying 'Did you know that you are 2.65 per cent over the wages budget for the period and 15.3 per cent over the energy budget'. Such 'inside information' was in the worst of cases used for what in Bass is known as KITA (kick in the arse) purposes. Thankfully, that is now behind us.

In Bass Taverns we now live in a managerial world of simultaneous and instantaneous information. All licensed house managers have a back office PC. They can get up-to-the-minute sales, costs and margins, productivity, stock and cash data. They are empowered via information to run their own businesses. All area managers have a lap-top PC and they can dial into the same EPOS and other databases and every corporate manager has a workstation on his or her desk. Information is now no longer power. But the ability to transform data into good information, to make better decisions really fast is a key goal. With shared information, important decisions can be made nearer to where it matters, and that is in the pub.

In Bass Taverns we have, or have developed information systems to support our core processes of operate pubs, develop pubs and manage cash. We also have information systems that support our teams, our targets and our plans.

Managers are still very much needed but we have seen their roles change. In the example of an area manager the role has changed as follows: they are process facilitators; they are coaches not controllers; they are business developers and not business 'doers'; they are team players not free-booters; they are adjudicators not hangmen; they remain great networkers, and networking skills for implementation and makings things happen, the driving forces that relate to that, are crucial.

As an organisation, we are less individualistic in our orientations and more team oriented and we certainly are more concerned with customers than we ever have been.

We need fewer managers. We have no supernumeraries at any level, which was not the case before. There is no room nor justification for such. Connector roles across processes is where middle managers are to be found, operating in an effective and value-adding manner.

Regarding empowering teams and how we set about it, just as for individuals, we wanted teams to do something powerful. We therefore had to give them something powerful to do. In Bass Taverns the most important role for the team of empowered licensed house managers is to produce a team business plan which is rooted in growing the business at the expense of competitors and not other Bass pubs. We have shown that such business planning activity really does bind the team together and make them act as one. Managers have had to become:

- supporters more than controllers
- developers of ideas and people
- forces for ongoing change.

An example of creative empowered decision making is the team of 'local pub' licensed house managers that entered into reciprocal trading arrangements with their multiscreen cinema complex neighbour. They encouraged their customers to use the complex at off-peak times by giving away discounted tickets with every meal bought in their pub, and the cinema in return offered cheap meal vouchers with every ticket bought at full price in the cinema. The team of licensed house managers produced their own 35mm slides using sophisticated PC software for advertising their outlets and their offers in the cinema, and all the cinema posters were shown in the pub. The really nice point about the story is that when the marketing managers of both companies were told of all this successful promotional activity they both came out with exactly the same comment ... 'They can't do that'! Our world is not perfect and some attitudes take longer to change, but we continue to work on those.

The Leicester Royal Infirmary – fundamental change for managers and management

Managing a process-driven organisation is fundamentally different to managing a functional one. The separate dimensions of clinical (at the level of the patient) and managerial (at the level of the process or function) accountability add to the complexity. The Leicester Royal Infirmary has only just begun to address many of the managerial issues. The re-engineering strategy involved a conscious decision to embark on the redesign of core healthcare processes before redesigning the organisational processes to support them. This has created some tensions. Some redesigned processes have had to be implemented without an obvious end-to-end management system to support them. Paradigms about management arrangements have been challenged, for instance, the concept that a process incorporating a specialist clinical service can only be managed by that specialist clinical service.

The managerial agenda is significant. Figure 6.1 shows at its core a clinical process being re-engineered. The outer segments typify the wider managerial and organisational issues that must be addressed. The very management process itself has to be re-engineered. The following conclusions have been drawn to date:

☐ Self-managed clinical process teams encompass both managerial and clinical responsibility. They require significantly less management and supervision than previous arrangements. One medical consultant has commented that following re-engineering his clinical team (including clinical and support staff) is meeting regularly to set objectives and monitor performance. This is the first time this has happened in his 20-year career.

☐ Accountability and responsibility are much better defined within re-engineered processes.

☐ The organisation's performance measurement framework must encompass targets at both a strategic and operational level. These are made up of a small number of key process measures which reflect success for the organisation as a whole. The targets and priorities of both individuals and clinical teams at all levels of the organisation should reflect these.

☐ Considerable time and effort must go into developing managers for new roles. This applies equally to senior management, middle management and clinical roles. People can't reorientate or develop new capabilities overnight. The same principles apply with self-managed teams. To create and sustain high performing self-managed teams takes much more than a few teambuilding sessions.

☐ In a healthcare environment the importance of involving clinical colleagues in the development of managerial and supervisory roles cannot be underestimated.

Figure 6.1

THE ROYAL LEICESTER INFIRMARY – MANAGEMENT ISSUES THAT MUST BE ADDRESSED IN RE-ENGINEERING A HEALTHCARE PROCESS

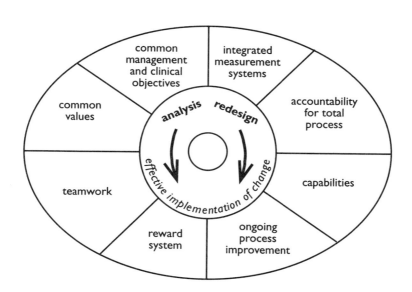

Some of the best role models for the new management have been senior clinical leaders within the hospital. They have recognised the potential of re-engineering for making changes in line with their own service vision. With support from the re-engineering teams, such clinical leaders have led much of the radical change within the organisation, skilfully avoiding many of the political minefields.

Rank Xerox – fundamental change for managers and management

The design team recommended that the new organisation should resemble the small units; about 400 employees in size, close to the customer, and with the best general managers at the head. These units had the virtues of simplicity, customer focus and, most importantly, employees felt part of their organisation. Communication and direction were easier to achieve in the small units. In the larger countries three to six customer business units (CBUs) were defined and implemented, while smaller countries were grouped into entities. The role of international and entity headquarters increasingly changed from direction to support; throughout the organisation the span of control increased, and the lines of communication were made shorter. The new organisation committed Rank Xerox to achieve the goals set by the CEO, and managers were in turn committed to their share of the improvements in the local organisations. There were reductions to be achieved, and Rank Xerox announced restructuring provisions to cover the cost of redundancies, which included staff at all levels. Managers and staff had to cope with the loss of colleagues, internal changes to organisations and relocation of departments to achieve productivity.

The most important long-term effect for managers and people was to extend personal responsibility and decision making. Each customer business unit was to be accountable for its results. This needed a new emphasis on effective business management, and leadership skills. More freedom was given to CBU managers and teams to take decisions on planning, customer contracts, pricing and service delivery. Business appreciation courses were delivered to help new managers develop.

Leadership courses were designed and implemented to develop existing and new managers. More teamworking was introduced, building on the existing self-managed work groups in service, and customer support teams to manage re-engineered business processes. Team skills training was essential in the implementation, so the new processes were not just overlaid onto the existing organisations, but merged with new behaviours and information flows. The role of managers in these new teams can be difficult. Most senior people developed as effective line managers, not as coaches, and the transition is not natural. The company is becoming more tolerant of mistakes, on the basis that risk taking will result in some failures – the important thing is to learn from them.

The human resource factors involved were thus increasingly important. HR developed criteria for selection of new managers, and new training programmes to improve the behavioural skills of all people. The concept of 360-degree appraisal was introduced in the training activity; before each course session, delegates gave anonymous questionnaires to their boss, their peers and their team. The comparison between these results and their own self-assessment was analysed with the help of a counsellor, and proved valuable in making people aware of their own style and where they needed to modify their approach.

It was recognised that new technologies and systems would eventually form an integral part of the new design, but it was possible to start initial implementation with existing information systems. Indeed, introducing all these changes simultaneously would have been a higher risk, and the lead time on systems delivery a significant delay to the benefits. This meant that the CBUs initially had to collect their own management information, and in some cases operate without the full range of systems support. People had to be self-reliant to get things done in the new environment.

The alignment to business process management is still developing. The new process architecture is well recognised, and high level metrics are in place. Process networks are responsible for all investment and systems decisions in their area of responsibility. Day-to-day operational emphasis on process management is less well developed, but is increasingly recognised as a necessary requirement. The introduction of redesigned processes has provided support here: initially they work well, providing a step-increase in performance, but they do require regular maintenance and attention to keep them working at peak performance, and improve further. The use of 'process coaches' in each CBU is developing to ensure this ongoing support.

The main emphasis on preparation for implementation in each entity was to create a unique plan for each area of geography, and ask for a local evaluation of the proposals. The solutions are not identical: the Nordic unit has a different structure to France, but the essential features of the design are in place in both entities. Local design and control of implementation was seen as key to local ownership of the activities, problems and results.

Royal Bank of Scotland – fundamental change for managers and management

In 1994, managing director Schofield launched an ambitious programme of communication focused entirely on his 'new deal' for staff. The change programme had, up to now, focused entirely on business processes – a number of pilots had been run, assessed, modified and run again. These were, however, limited in nature and, as a consequence, few staff were aware of the wholesale changes to come.

The Columbus HR team or 'solution space' providers were, between October 1993 and January 1994, frantically redefining the nature of work in the new bank to match the redesigned business process which had earlier been piloted in the branch network. However, for sustained, meaningful and impactful change, it was never going to be enough just to write a whole series of job descriptions to match the new business processes. What was needed for the change programme to succeed, was a radical reappraisal of all the core HR processes. In February 1994, the HR team accompanied Schofield on a nationwide tour to brief managers and staff through the cascade process on the proposed changes. However, before they could do so it had been essential to redefine the fundamentals of HR as it had previously been carried out in the bank. The HR team recognised, as the results of the pilot projects and process redesign work were being analysed, that one thing was inevitable – the nature of work and careers in the bank would never be the same again.

At a change management group presentation to directors of the Retail Bank and the board of Westpack, the Australian banking group (who were on a benchmarking visit) in late November 1993, the HR team put forward their analysis which required the directors' commitment to a much more explicit proposition to the bank's staff. Up to this point staff had been told things were going to be different but very little flesh had been put on the bones. What emerged from this presentation was a document titled *New Roles in a New Bank*. In the introduction to the document it stated: 'This brochure describes most of the New Roles in the branch network together with their activities and responsibilities. For each role, possible development opportunities are described and the level of experience and skills likely to be required are indicated.' It went on, 'The roles must be seen within the context of the principles and commitments set out in *New Roles in a New Bank*. The Directors of the Retail Bank are committing to building the framework to make the new roles a reality. There has been uncertainty and this is one of the first steps in clarifying the future. Making it work will require the introduction of new processes and systems, particularly for appraisal, career development and training.'

New Roles in a New Bank mapped out how the new business processes would become a reality by describing the work. What was made explicit for the first time was that no longer were there to be generalist careers in banking, the business had been redesigned around critical customer-serving processes, not around functions, technologies or geographies. In doing so the bank was essentially rewriting the psychological contract, particularly for managers. The managers had been brought up in a world where their perspective was, 'If I work hard and am loyal to the organisation, I will always have a job and the organisation will take care of me'. From a manager's perspective this usually meant 'I can also expect regular promotions throughout my career with ever-increasing status and benefits.'

In February 1994, the Bank essentially revoked this psychological contract and replaced it with an explicit architecture for

HR (Figure 6.2). On implementation, the new HR processes implied a new psychological contract based on performance, contribution and careers based on building specialist expertise. This model and the underlying processes explained how the new deal of *New Roles in a New Bank* was to become a reality, and is based on the concept of the whole being greater than the sum of the parts. Architecture on paper alone is nothing but a pretty picture unless there is substance behind it. Over an 18-month period the HR team developed the conceptual model or architecture then proceeded to build from scratch the substance, in the form of entirely new processes and practices for each element of the model. This involved applying the process redesign model illustrated in Figure 5.1, which required designing, testing and implementing, together with being able to demonstrate positive net present value (NPV) for each element.

Job and organisation design

Jobs were described using a competency model that focused not only on what had to be done but also on how. Furthermore, it was critical to describe the linkages between roles and how careers could be developed in this new era of specialisation. The HR team saw this element as the fundamental building block – almost the DNA of human resource management. If we could describe both the 'what' and the 'how' of work, together with the linkages, then there was a much better chance of having impactful HR processes and strategies.

Figure 6.2

ROYAL BANK OF SCOTLAND – MODEL FOR AN INTEGRATED HR ARCHITECTURE

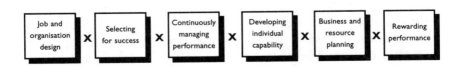

= High-performing and capable organisation

Selecting for success

Selection had, in the past, been a matter of knowing the right people. This was no longer to be the case; having described the new roles it was critical to ensure the best person for the role was appointed. Therefore, when implementing the new bank processes, all managers were given the opportunity to apply for a new role. A rigorous criterion- or competency-based selection process was implemented that ensured consistency, fairness and objectivity.

The process was 'cascaded' through the organisation. As new top management teams were selected by the directors, they were first trained in using criterion-based interviews and then selected their own teams using the same process. No one was allowed to interview unless they were successful in the practical training programme. Furthermore, a key component in the selection process was the redefinition of managerial work and then selecting not only for technical ability but also the capacity to lead, develop and coach others. As a consequence we were, through the selection process, reinforcing the core management practices and values in the new bank.

An assessed quality line was set and, rather than make compromise appointments, vacancies were left open. The selection process therefore became the guardian of the integrity of the change programme. It also allowed both more women to come through into managerial roles and a detailed analysis of the core competence of the bank's staff, laying the foundation of a worthwhile human asset register.

Continuously managing performance

A new performance management system was designed and implemented which linked both inputs and outputs for each role. For the first time a coherent picture was created of how each role and process was mutually supporting. The performance management system links each individual with business and unit strategies and is both a top-down and bottom-up process, allowing the individual to influence direction. Furthermore, every manager has been trained in applying the system and every member of staff has also been trained in how to get the most from the new process. This is a paradigm shift. In the old bank, managers set direction and imposed the process; in today's competitive world we need total participation. Furthermore, performance measurement and management was no longer a once a year ritual, driven by HR, but a key business process owned by and usually implemented by line managers and their staff.

Developing individual capability

Early on the HR team recognised that the bank's 'spray and pray' approach to training and development was no longer appropriate. Training had to be specific and related to maximising performance in the new roles. Rather than predominantly being centre based it was now to be taken into the business and delivered 'just-in-time'. As new teams were appointed, so too was their specific and immediate training. Longer term development based on individual need was also identified via the selection process and this was addressed in ways that were impactful for the individual, taking account of learning style and preference. For each role described in *New Roles in a New Bank* a complementary development and training programme was also identified which outlined not only structured programmes, but also on the job activities.

Business and resource planning

Business and resource planning is the integrating module of the new performance management system that creates a human asset register for the business, in so doing allowing realistic HR planning to take place. It is also the vehicle for assessing business goals against the human resources who will have to achieve them.

Rewarding for success

In the past, people made a number of job moves to essentially 'grade hop'. In doing so, they were able to increase their base salary and this reinforced the generalist banker career profile. Very early on the HR team recognised that longevity in a role was critical to our success because customers were demanding increasing levels of expertise. Therefore, new reward structures had to be put in place that allowed for salary progression without changing roles. However, it was also recognised that the absence of the other elements in the HR architecture would make apply-

ing any new reward processes difficult, if not impossible. Therefore the HR architecture is multiplicative; if any one element is
missing, a zero sum results. However, by integrating all the core
HR processes in this way, we are able to ensure coherence,
consistency and ultimately enhance the credibility of the HR
function to make the change programme a reality.

Toshiba – fundamental change for managers and management

There were to be some pretty fundamental changes. No one,
including managers, was to have a job description. Most of the
barriers that management can hide behind were to be removed;
there were to be no physical barriers of separate offices for
managers, from the managing director downwards. Information was to be openly available to everyone; not guarded and
'traded' by individuals holding functionally specific information. There were to be no distinguishing features such as those
relating to different forms of dress for different categories of
employees; all, from the managing director downwards, would
wear the same coats and would be distinguished only by a
name badge which would not indicate job function, department or job title. Dining facilities, working hours and
employee benefits were to be common. The organisation structure was to be extremely 'flat'; little hierarchy and with few
levels from the bottom of the organisation to the managing
director. Someone asked, 'What, indeed, will distinguish
managers?' The answer was, 'The capability to manage.'

The difficulties were (a) how to define what managers' roles
and responsibilities were, and (b) how to engender the appropriate skills and behaviours in managers. In terms of how to
define managers' roles, this stemmed largely from an expression of 'outputs'. Top management were notionally accountable
for discreet functions but collectively responsible for organisational outputs. It was not defined, but in this structure
individuals did not make decisions on their own. Collective
responsibility facilitated collective involvement and, on decisions affecting employees, employees were, through the
processes that were set up (particularly the advisory board),
consulted before decisions were to be taken.

At departmental and section level, some communications procedures were specifically defined. Managers and section leaders were required, every morning, to hold a five-minute meeting with the employees in the section; not some mornings, *every* morning.

Individuals, at the individual level, and groups at the group level were to have accountability for their work. Individual production operatives were to have their individual performance in quality terms fed back to them and displayed for their reference and action immediately above their workplace. This was, of course, available for anyone else to see. Work was organised so that individual tasks and roles would be known and allocated; not by some remote department but by each team leader who could take into account 'local' needs and issues. Complex programming operations to ensure correct sequence for insertion of parts in automatic insertion machines was to be undertaken by the machine operators themselves; not by a remote department or outside contractor. Supervision was to become a combination of specialist technical support and advice, co-ordination and encouragement, coupled with overall accountability for group performance and company operating standards including attendance, timekeeping, discipline, etc.

Group, as well as individual, performance was made visible on notice boards, etc., within sections. Daily, weekly and monthly performance against a variety of dimensions was plotted by employees in the section. There is nothing very special about these processes but what was different was the way in which people were involved. It wasn't so much about what people did as about how they felt about doing it. The essence was to get people feeling involved not just being involved. This was not an easy process to achieve; not everyone wanted to feel involved. Some just wanted to do a job and get paid. A few managers, despite careful selection and training, didn't naturally take to the new egalitarian ways. Some felt that it wasn't always necessary to have a five-minute morning meeting; others decided that it was much easier and quicker to make decisions and tell people what to do. But the system had been designed for a purpose and proved sufficiently powerful to effect its own controls and ultimately bring about a change in behaviour.

The company advisory board became a powerful influence, not on individual issues, but upon adherence to the principles if one part of the organisation seemed to be going its own way. Its role was and is as a guardian and adviser. Its role was not limited in any way other than *not* being empowered to discuss matters relating to individuals.

Overall, the major task was breaking down traditional attitudes. This was coupled with the inclination and capacity of people to taking detailed or sophisticated information and to understand its implications, particularly when they have previously been taught that such information is not their concern but that of management, and where management have been trained to believe it was their concern. Barriers had to be broken down on all sides. It took some time to readjust and in particular for managers to settle into their new roles as coach and leader rather than controller and director. Without job descriptions these requirements were implicit rather than explicit; it just took time and a lot of open reviews.

The main difficulty in all of this was how to balance the requirements of the finely tuned batch production system requiring detailed planning and logistical control with a sense of involvement and capability for contribution from individuals and groups. Manufacturing televisions, however organised, involves many repetitive processes and is considered by most to be pretty boring. Other variables were therefore introduced to help limit difficulties arising: job rotation, new job training/development, etc. Toshiba employees would probably not feel that they were working in 'empowered teams' but they would certainly notice from experience in working in other organisations that the style of work, openness and scope for individual as well as collective involvement was a much higher level. Also, that management processes were more 'hands off' rather than 'hands on'.

In summary, no sophisticated means were used to achieve the new standards and ways of working. Results were obtained more by expression of the overall required standards and open policing of them. The outcome was ultimately a 'settling in' to a new style.

7

MANAGING REWARDS

☐ Without changes in reward systems, major change cannot be accomplished successfully.

☐ There are essential rewards that have nothing to do with money.

☐ A reward strategy and reward systems need to be adopted that support changed behaviours, serve internal and external customers' needs and enhance co-operation.

☐ Team and individual rewards are both important.

☐ Management of reward systems increasingly needs to be appropriately delegated.

☐ Reward initiatives are never wholly stand-alone; they must be aligned to the business and wider HR strategies.

☐ Designing reward systems requires professional capability.

Reward systems mostly develop over time, being the output of national, regional, local and individual influences and impacts. They have been the product of different and sometimes opposing vested interests. They are compromises or impositions, evolving from a succession of conflicting tensions. They have been usually designed for a specific purpose and for a particular group of employees at a particular time.

Rewards must change

Without changes in reward systems, major organisational change will not be acomplished. Given a big shift in the division of work activity across traditional functions and levels, then it is certain that hitherto existing reward systems will need to change. If they do not change, to be compatible with what might be entirely new ways of work structure and organisation, there will be an inclination for the behaviours influenced by the system to continue. Any required behaviours in new work processes will be undermined. People will tend to return to traditional habits.

The imposition of major change will, itself, cause the issue of reward, particularly 'pay', to be brought into sharp relief. Reward systems do, though, go well beyond issues of pay. A reward system can be described as: 'Any conscious intervention or series of interventions within an organisation aimed at encouraging or reinforcing required behaviours, or which compensate people for taking particular actions.'

The nature of rewards in re-engineering

A reward system may be formal or informal, related to monetary reward or otherwise, and be immediate or delayed (or all of them). Whatever a system's nature, if the base that it serves fundamentally changes, then it too will need to change. A company's business strategy will determine the appropriate human resource management strategies, which will nearly always include more than one reward strategy. Different interventions will be needed to provide (a) support for actually bringing about changed behaviours, and (b) support for maintenance of changed behaviours.

In most surveys that categorise an 'order of priorities' that people want from work, rarely is money highest in the hierarchy of needs. Reward strategies are not only about money, they are about both tangible and intangible forms of reward. Tangible rewards will include money and a wider range of benefits that may be equated to money. However, intangible rewards, like acknowledgement and praise, also have an important place. Rewards can be categorised according to the outcomes. The required or anticipated outcomes are needed to be known in order to design and manage any new reward system. The following two kinds of reward intervention are set to provide encouraging or positive behaviours:

☐ positive reinforcement – when people receive something of value for what they have contributed

☐ negative reinforcement – when a person needs to act to avoid something unacceptable or unpleasant.

Positive reinforcement can be acknowledgement from a boss or team, promotion, one-off bonuses or awards and awards for achievement of a specific goal (though non-achievement which brings no reward can act as a punishment and as a demotivator). The possibility of unpleasant or unacceptable consequences, such as loss of a job or chance of promotion, which may be implied rather than expressed, is perhaps more widely used than many understand and the consequences can work both ways; an 'awkward' employee might be given a higher performance rating by a boss to avoid either public acknowledgement that his staff are underperforming or in order to avoid confrontation with the disaffected employee. There are other interventions that are set to discourage rather encourage certain behaviours:

- [ ] punishment – when individuals receive undesired attention for something they have not done, as required
- [ ] omission – when people don't receive something they were expecting as a result of a positive contribution that they have made, or consider they have made.

In 'omission', isolation is felt when, for example, 'for operational reasons', reward is withdrawn by management, such as 'As the performance was achieved because of favourable foreign exchange movements, it will not be paid' (one author's sharply remembered experience, having had an earlier bonus not paid owing to adverse foreign exchange movements!). This sort of intervention can be perceived as 'unjust', and be wholly demotivating if there were no such provisions mentioned beforehand. The simple case of managers not acknowledging or even noticing a good effort or performance is a common oversight. Whether or not it is a conscious omission, the effect will be the same.

Encouraging voluntarism
A complex amalgam of positive and negative forces exist in all work environments to a greater or lesser extent; more typically symbolised as 'sticks and carrots'. Individuals, consciously or unconsciously, are taking action because of the consequences of operating within their existing system. Positive reinforcements are the only interventions that encourage people to take

actions because they *want* to. Positive reinforcements are the only interventions that encourage people to do something in an entirely voluntary way. If people of their own volition want to respond, they will feel much more part of the intervention and, hence, more satisfied with the outcome.

Like all other initiatives that an organisation can take to more readily bring about dramatic change, reward systems are about encouraging or reinforcing changes in behaviour support-ive to the organisation's goals and helping to perpetuate effective behaviour. But they cannot safely be designed just on a task-by-task or process-by-process basis, owing to the tensions that can be created between elements within the total system. So, what is a positive reinforcer in one area or for one group of employees can be a negative force against other needs or expectations. For example, paying a salesperson extremely highly for specified results may be contrary to what some (not only those with personal vested interests) may consider 'fair'.

Choice

Individuals and teams in an organisation that has undergone business process re-engineering will probably be required to be much more self-directed in the context of work that they undertake, making judgements, etc. In these circumstances, it might be incongruous or even counterproductive to have wholly imposed reward structures. Greater scope for initiative in the workplace admits the need to think about the degree of choice that employees might be given to exercise judgement about the composition of their rewards. This can range, for example, from participation in the design of pay systems to selection by individuals under a 'cafeteria'-type structure from a range of pay and benefits, within a given value.

Enhancing collaboration

All organisations have customers of some kind (internal and external) and the reward systems need to help further efforts for serving all those customers. Again, as with the example of the highly paid salesperson, some reward-related interventions will have a tendency to hinder rather than enhance collabora-tion. The optimal reward system will support:

1   positive impacts on behaviour
2   focus upon serving internal and external customers
3   enhanced co-operation within the organisation.

Ideally what is needed, is a system that *encourages* employees (whether employed directly, or in some outsourced employment, including subcontractors and suppliers). Although this book is primarily focused on 'employees', the 'insides' of organisations during re-engineering sometimes move 'outside'. People notionally external to the organisation but who provide goods or services supportive to the organisation need their 'reward' systems appropriately designed, just as much as any 'internal' employee. With Toshiba, involving suppliers in the forward business planning and advising them immediately of known or anticipated variations, together with an underpinning undertaking to accept a product which had been ordered, together with a guarantee to pay their bills promptly and within a very short time-scale, led to more positive and supportive actions from them.

Overall the newer, more flexible, organisations engaging employee involvement in processes, in perhaps a much more responsive way, rather than a series of predetermined tasks, demands new thinking. For their reward systems to be compatible with the behaviours that they are expecting in the workplace, they ideally need to move towards a win/win outcome for the organisation and its employees – to move from a 'have to' environment to a 'want to' environment.

Performance management

The new paradigm within organisations demands increasing attention to the complex and interlocking processes involved in performance management. Performance management is much, much more than the introduction of such tools as performance appraisals. Indeed, one of the authors has for much of his career been inhibiting pressures for what he considered to be inappropriate forms of employee appraisal. Few people believe that performance appraisal systems are working to the extent wished for and the emergence of new practices and processes of working will demand a fundamental reconsideration of an organisation's appraisal systems, outputs and processes.

Simplification and delegation of performance management processes to much lower and wider levels than hitherto with fewer formal procedures results in more action taken because people 'want to' rather than 'have to' at every level. If there is to be greater accountability for performance management down the line, greater clarity of organisational goals and customer needs will have to be brought about. Organisational goals will need to be translated at operational levels into goals which are meaningful to people involved in the process of delivery. Measuring processes rather than tasks might at first appear more difficult but measuring them is critical to equitable and focused outputs.

More empowered performance management processes are themselves more difficult to manage yet they do need managing, from the centre. Delegation does not mean abrogation of accountability. Measures relating to total organisational performance, sectional performance and individual performance need to be made visible.

Especially within more dynamic organisations, feedback (both complimentary and critical) needs to be given in a timely and positively reinforcing way. If, for example, an employee is doing something which is patently unsafe, it would be inappropriate to wait until a performance appraisal one year hence to counsel the employee about the potential danger to him- or herself and the consequences upon immediate colleagues and the organisation as a whole. Where an employee goes out of their way to help another, resulting in an improved performance within a section, it would again be inappropriate to wait for perhaps another year to provide positive feedback. The more those involved can share such issues and make them visible in a timely way, the more rewarding those actions will be for both the individuals and the organisation.

Integrating rewards with strategy

Earlier in this chapter (see page 141) we identified the need for supporting actions in order to bring about change as well as supportive action for the continuum systems. They need to be managed together; not to follow from each other but only so far that they do not undermine each other. Reward for helping to develop a re-engineered organisation, based upon the successful outcomes, is an important consideration to help bring about change. Monetary-related reward will nevertheless not be sufficient on its own. Reward (both positive reinforcement reward and negative reinforcement reward) can be considered for all participants. Participants might include activists in project management teams, participants in the re-engineered workplace and any 'casualties' that may emerge but whose co-operation is nevertheless required. Note that the reward for casualties is not only for their benefit. If 'survivors' do not see casualties being treated in ways that they consider are fair and equitable, negative reactions will emerge to a greater extent than would otherwise be the case.

Such rewards for everyone need to be planned well in advance, considering all of the implications and then communicated clearly and simply. Such communication should not be cluttered with 'justification'; that will merely provide 'fog'. If there is to be a monetary reward which is on a sliding scale, this must be made clear. Addressing difficulties that arise subsequently will induce insecurity.

Positive participation in re-engineering by, eg project team members, will include perceived exposure to risk. Those risks must be acknowledged and addressed. Be specific; don't rely on the potentially misinterpreted and sometimes broken promises of 'Trust me', or 'I'll see you alright'.

Rewards for reinforcement

The options for providing reinforcement fall into four main groups:

☐ work-related, eg promotion, development opportunity, special assignment, greater responsibility, opportunity to implement own idea

☐ money-related, eg lump-sum payments/awards (one off), increased salary, stock options, additional money-related benefits not paid as cash such as enhanced pension, extended insurance cover

☐ symbolism-related – a tangible prize (eg cup or plaque), a bigger chair, a certificate for, eg 'challenging the system and living to tell about it'(!), a small party where the awardee is guest of honour

☐ personal, eg simply saying 'thank you', face to face, by phone or in a letter (or a combination) from immediate boss or top management.

While directly work-related and money-related rewards are important, the value of more personal and symbolic rewards should never be underestimated. One of the authors especially remembers the impact on him years ago of his boss saying, after a particularly gruelling project, 'Thanks very much for a job well done. I know your wife hasn't seen much of you lately; please take her out to dinner [at a very expensive restaurant] with my compliments'. Those thanks carried through into family life paid dividends for years hence. However, symbols, powerful as they are, need to be considered carefully and selected appropriately. The yellow jersey awarded to the leader in the *Tour de France* cycle race may be an inappropriate symbol when team effort is required.

Timely reinforcement

Providing timely reinforcement in an open and sincere way whether to subordinates, work-colleagues, supervisors and top management (not forgetting internal and external customers and suppliers), there is an opportunity to generate practices that build positive reinforcement into everyday life. A bonus received at the end of a period will be all the more meaningful to an individual or group who understand their perhaps small but vital contribution towards the achievement that generated that bonus. The timing of rewards can sometimes make all the difference. Thanks should be 'JIT (just in time) thanks' – too late and the point will be missed. They should be specific so that the recipient knows to what they are related. Wherever possible, they should be personalised. Also, rewards that are given when they are not expected can perceptively pay many times the face value but, of their nature, these cannot provide an incentive before an event.

Team versus individual incentives

'Individual' versus 'team' reward is always an issue of balance between the two. Where effective teamworking becomes a behaviour which is desired (whenever wasn't it?!), then reward related to the required behaviour, as much as a more measurable product or service output, should be considered.

A guide to focusing incentive-related reward is use (with minor variations) of the SMART acronym.

☐ Specific – specific to the organisation's needs and the behaviours required to bring them about
☐ Meaningful – where the reward is appropriate to the value delivered and the context of the situation
☐ Achievable – goals should not be too difficult to achieve and can be stage-related with 'pay-outs' at intermediate stages, building to a 'total success' payout requiring real 'stretch'. Goals that are perceived to be unattainable won't be attempted by some. Providing feedback on progress and stage payments can bring a seemingly distant horizon much nearer.
☐ Reliable – rewards have to be made in line with the agreed 'rules' or framework agreed or explained. Moving the 'goal-posts' will guarantee negative behaviour.
☐ Timely – the relationship between actual start, achievement and award, needs to be finely balanced, with awards being made as soon after achievement as possible.

Reward strategy trends

It is not within the capability of this book to provide solutions for every eventuality nor can it outline all of the options. All we can hope to do is to provide some signposts highlighting the needs/options for alternative strategies. Strategies suitable for ongoing stable times, times of dramatic change and ongoing continual change need to be different to the particular circumstances. The trends are towards:

☐ devolvement (away from central control)
☐ tailored around processes (away from structured systems)
☐ person evaluation; competence and contribution related (away from over-reliance on pseudo-scientific job evaluation)
☐ line management held tools (away from personnel department ownership)

☐ performance management related (away from performance assessment related)

☐ self-directed development related (away from training programme related)

☐ performance improvement related (away from length of service related)

☐ core and out-sourced employee related (away from long-term employment)

Reward system trends

Entirely new kinds of reward systems, different than those applied hitherto (such as in a stairway of overlapping grades) are emerging. These include the following.

Competency-based structures

This is where capabilities are defined at each level and rewards benchmarked to the market, then applied, perhaps, on a 'job family' basis, where the boss has scope to allocate rewards appropriate to that family. This has a holistic approach and relates contribution to relative competence in the market-place, but families within an organisation may differ between functions. With families, however, mobility across the organisation can be restricted, militating against the application of cross-functional processes and even change itself. It requires new understanding, skills and accountabilities by line managers to be managed well.

Broad banding

This is where bands (grades) span perhaps two or three previous grade levels, resulting in the upper pay levels being perhaps more than twice the bottom pay levels. In broad-banded approaches, promotion will be less frequent and therefore less visible. Market pay information is used more flexibly as a guide to positioning. It demands higher standards of management within overall budgets. Broad banding can link with competence based applications.

Skill based

This is where pay increases are in line with the number of skills acquired. This aids acquisition of both depth and breadth of skills and more flexible application of those skills, but is generally not suitable for knowledge-related jobs such as those in management. It is dependent upon high access to training opportunities and the organisation needs to consider how to manage redundant skills.

Toshiba applied a skills-based pay structure for its manufacturing and support operatives, eg those in the factory, in the stores and in the offices. Management and professional employees were dealt with more along the lines of broad banding.

External factors

Some situations can be extremely complex, as in the case of The Leicester Royal Infirmary, where there are considerable externally induced tensions relating to pay. National unions indicate their wish to maintain national pay bargaining but this is contrary to re-engineering wisdom for making rewards appropriate to required outputs. Through re-engineering, roles and 'outputs' may be quite different, in one locality compared with another. This conundrum will have to be ultimately resolved at national level. There are however some signs of preference for 'local' rather than national terms and conditions, where the option can be offered. The high level of involvement of staff in all aspects of re-engineering may contribute to this trend. A debate on the issue will no doubt continue.

Holistic issues

It should be reinforced that, whatever systems are adopted, there should be a strong operational/business exigency behind them. The systems mentioned above will not necessarily be applied on a discrete basis but mixing and matching may be appropriate. Whatever, they should be focused on the required behaviours. The systems should also take into account the holistic perspective within the organisation. If variety rather than conformity is to be the name of the game then this must become explicit within the organisation. The conflicting 'pulls' towards conformity on the one hand and variety on the other need to be considered with great care and the relative tensions balanced.

The roles required to be played by the reward systems need to be identified and the mechanisms provided to manage the systems to be adopted. All systems need management. Management takes resources, both in terms of information, including central advice (internal or external) and skills and knowledge.

Changes in attitude throughout the organisation at every level, and spanning former functions will be required. These have to be planned and budgeted for. People within the organisation have to know and to accept that what might be a major change is important and 'for real'. Major change within a reward system will bring about similar reactions to any other change. Changes in reward systems are a subset of business process re-engineering in the wider sense. People must understand the reasons for change, they must be drawn to understand the vision of what the new processes will help bring about. Once they understand these they will need to be prepared and involved for implementation.

Like other aspects of re-engineering, top management support is critical to all reward initiatives and top management behaviour, by example, will help reinforce these. There are notable examples of top executives taking what are perceived to be disproportionate rewards, even if the 'market intelligence' supports those awards. In such circumstances, negative consequences elsewhere in the organisation have to be accounted for. In all circumstances, communication is vital.

Bass Taverns – managing rewards

Bass have generally tried to adopt a philosophy of rewarding people for what they do, not what they say they do. This calls for measurement.

Bass Taverns, concurrent with the re-engineering activities, introduced a new approach to the management of performance and reward for corporate staff. This emphasised flexibility beyond earlier more rigid approaches. The new approach was conditioned by the unprecedented changes within the hospitality retailing industry, the need for a highly competitive and distinctive environment with encouragement to achieve new types of goal and what, through a survey, employees said about the then existing salary, grading and benefit structures.

During the series of 200 structured interviews that comprised the employee survey, the employees indicated that:

- the existing grading structure was not seen as a motivating factor. Indeed, there was little common understanding of the structure
- there did not appear to be a direct enough relationship between the actual level of individual performance and the level of salary increases. The objective setting and appraisal process was not considered to be very effective
- while basic salaries were generally considered to be competitive, there was a feeling among staff that some greater flexibility should be offered on benefits
- there was an overwhelming view that the salary policy and structure should be communicated in a more open and effective manner.

The new approach was piloted in one area of the company and then adopted as a new overall framework, with:

- One salary structure for both corporate and clerical staff, to replace earlier separate structures covering corporate staff, trade management staff and a variety of regional clerical schemes.
- Three broad categories – 'divisional resource' (having significant divisional impact), 'management' (qualified or specialist including management of people, assets and policies) and 'professional' (day-to-day activity implementing decisions, providing information, etc.).
- One method of job evaluation.
- New bonus and incentive programmes – to widen and enhance opportunity for improved earnings through improved performance.
- Realigned benefits within a broad category.
- Benefits for cash – an opportunity for company car users to trade down in favour of a cash supplement.
- A commitment to coaching and managing performance aimed at ensuring that individuals can develop their competencies, qualifications and careers.

Individual salaries are determined by looking at a combination of job size (determined by job evaluation), comparative market value and individual performance for similar jobs. As the new categories are very broad, there are not fixed minimum or maximum salaries for each category, and no personal salary thresholds.

Most of the re-engineering work in Bass Taverns has resulted in the formation of teams to tackle operational or development opportunities. This has demanded addressing team- as well as individual-related pay. Quite often these teams are cross-functional, interdisciplinary, of mixed sex and age groups, often they range considerably in terms of grade and salary and in most cases the teams have to perform a key task or deliver new products or services. Teamworking is critical; meeting demanding targets is a requirement. Such new ways of working and reward systems that are rooted in individual performance may seem strange bedfellows; certain performance management policies including performance-related pay could be divisive and counter-productive in the context of the team and its new way of working. Bass devised a whole range of team rewards and incentives to cope with the exigency. We would never claim that team rewards must inevitably take over from individual performance-related pay in all circumstances but we would say that where you have a team delivering measurable outputs along agreed milestones then team reward systems are essential.

One pay example involved acquisition and development teams who were working in entirely new ways. We rewarded these teams on the basis of team performance and, for just about doubling their output across the key performance indicators, they were rewarded with substantial bonuses. That solution may be obvious, but how similarly to reward a team of trainers implementing a new IT system is not so straightforward.

In another case of trainers, we had no easy answers but we followed a similar philosophy, Bass got:

☐ delegates on courses to rate their experience
☐ delegates on courses to rate the trainer
☐ delegates on courses to complete exams and other tests of competence

☐ delegates to rate the coaching skills of trainers on follow-up coaching sessions on the job.

We gave participants further tests of competence. Finally, we measured whether the IT system was delivering benefits against the original cost-benefit specification, and whether the 'milestones' were being met. On this basis of measurement, we rewarded the team. We then got team members to rate team members to ensure there was an internal feeling of 'felt fairness'.

Neither of these two team incentive systems is perfect, but in the early stages of BPR we were prepared to accept imperfections in order to encourage new ways of working.

In the context of teams and team reward, a wonderful sanction can be mentioned that is only available to teams of equals in dealing with an underperforming team member. That sanction is social pressure, usually delivered by gossip. If an individual believes that their performance is being talked about in a group of equals round the organisational equivalent of a camp fire, this can be a powerful motivator. Nevertheless, open and accepted peer appraisal processes built into the system can provide more orderly and perhaps fairer means of achieving similar outcomes with less potential for adverse effects.

The Leicester Royal Infirmary – managing rewards

The development of reward systems which reflect the competencies, skills and behaviours required in a process-focused organisation is the cornerstone of any re-engineering programme. However, as a public sector organisation we are grappling with complexity which organisations in other sectors do not face.

Within the National Health Service there is a tradition of central negotiation for pay and conditions. The establishment of NHS Trusts created scope for local pay and conditions. However, local pay determination is very much opposed by trade unions at the national level. This creates an inherent tension. An example was the situation earlier in The Leicester Royal Infirmary re-engineering programme, where local trade union representatives found themselves faced with the local management desire to develop a reward system for re-engineered systems. This was in direct conflict with the national trade union agenda. The central conflict has to be resolved at a national level. However, The Leicester Royal Infirmary staff are moving into redefined job-roles. They have the option of Trust rather than National terms and conditions, and most of them are choosing the local option.

As job roles are redesigned and performance measurement frameworks developed, reward systems will continue to be a crucial part of the re-engineering agenda. The BPR programme offers the opportunity to reward additional responsibilities undertaken by staff working within re-engineered processes. In future, reward systems may cover:

☐ contribution towards the *strategic direction* – in terms of both process and clinical outcomes
☐ reward for skills and role development
☐ teamwork, as a stated performance measurement objective.

Rank Xerox – managing rewards

Rank Xerox already had a system of rewards linked to business performance, with a growing proportion of variable pay. During the 1980s pay was increasingly linked to achievement of corporate priorities, with a significant bonus for customer satisfaction paid to all staff, managers rewarded on return on assets, and employee satisfaction results also contributed. A recognition policy provided personal awards for excellence, and were widely available to individuals and teams.

The new design extended these policies, and enabled customer business units (CBUs) to act with more flexibility in setting goals and rewards. Team-based pay was extended to allow administrative staff to share in their contribution to the success of sales teams. Service teams began to experiment with self-management of pay reviews. Initial results showed that people were more satisfied with the allocation of pay when they participated in the review, even when the average pay rise was the same in other teams.

Through the surveys, employees could comment on their satisfaction with pay and recognition, and these results were now available at team level. Team leaders responded with more specific actions to improve the overall level of satisfaction. The growing need for advanced skills in technology and leadership was obvious, and work is in progress on the development of skills-based pay.

Every member of Rank Xerox had an annual appraisal and participated in a review process to select potential development candidates. This process was extended to ensure that everyone was assessed against a list of leadership attributes and values, where competence is mandatory for further progression, and where training emphasises the development of these skills.

The results, shown in Table 7.1, gave good impetus to the new organisation, and everyone shared in the success.

Table 7.1

RANK XEROX RESULTS AFTER ONE YEAR

	1993	1994
Customer satisfaction	91%	95%
Employee satisfaction	Country norm	70% > norm
Market share	Current	10% revenue growth
Return on assets	7%	13%

Royal Bank of Scotland – managing rewards

At an early stage of the human resources process redesign, it was realised that substantial changes would have to be made to reward practice. Like many large organisations, the Royal Bank had adopted the Hay job evaluation methodology for valuing work. As a result of applying job evaluation criteria to size jobs, primarily know how or knowledge required to do the work, problem solving or the complexity of the issues faced by the job holder, together with accountability in terms of assets and people managed, the bank created a complex hierarchy modelled on military command and control structures.

As with other large organisations in both the USA and Europe during the immediate post-war years, right up until the oil crisis of the 1970s and the stock market crash of the late

1980s, there was felt to be little need to challenge the basic design and structure of organisations. However, increasing global competition, cash crisis, pressure on costs and the emergence of a new management credo of the mid 1980s put forward by, among others, Tom Peters and Robert Waterman in their book *In Search of Excellence*, challenged the basis and need for command and control hierarchies staffed by legions of managers.

The redesign of managerial work focused on greater specialisation and, for those in customer-facing roles, the need to build relationships over a longer time frame. This meant that the previous regime of frequent job changes to chase grades and therefore increase base salary had to be addressed if we were to make the new organisation work. Furthermore, analysis of the new roles using detailed competency models meant that the old evaluation criteria largely driven by 'what' had to be done, became obsolete. The competency framework gave a far greater sense of 'how' work needed to be performed and therefore introduced an additional measurement dimension that focused on behaviour as well as output.

The former 'psychological contract' was based on frequent job moves, for example the career-aspired manager could expect to move every 18–24 months. If we wanted managers, once they had been selected, to remain in their new roles for longer then a fresh approach to reward had to be taken. In particular we needed to be able to reward achievement, application of the new competencies and demonstration of the new behaviours such as coaching, leadership and customer orientation. Reward systems, by definition, should be designed to encourage desired outputs and behaviours; all too often, however, they fail to do so. The design of a coherent architecture for HR processes was based on a 'systems' approach, whereby all elements of the system are interdependent.

By clearly defining our expectations for each 'new role' in a 'new bank', and by developing a complementary performance management system that focused on both the 'what' and the 'how' of work, more reliable measurement metrics could be established. Furthermore, by more clearly articulating the linkages between the roles, it was possible for the first time to connect individuals to business plans and ultimately business strategy. These linkages allowed for far greater levels of differentiation, which meant that it became possible to measure absolute performance and individual value added. With clearer definition of expectation and accompanying measurement metrics we moved away from 'vanilla' reward practice and began to build on earlier experience of introducing higher levels of variable pay to reward both outputs such as achieving revenue targets and behaviours, for example increasing customer satisfaction.

Following detailed analysis of total reward practice, it was decided to introduce fewer but broader pay bands and standardise benefits. This would allow competent individuals to be rewarded for performance within their new role and obviate the need for the frequent job changes of the past. For some roles it has been possible to introduce higher levels of variable pay to reward the achievement of particular key result areas, for example profitability and the underlying objectives which could include elements of revenue and cost management.

Integrating the reward system within the framework of the HR architecture ensured reward became a critical element in the selection process. A booklet, *New Roles in a New Bank*, described not only the content of the jobs but also the bank's overall proposition to its staff, together with the framework for reward. An element of self-selection was introduced when staff began applying for the new roles. Together with the published material on jobs, reward and selection, the bank was also able to hold 'job fairs' at which new job incumbents could describe their roles to colleagues. Together these elements combined to provide a realistic preview of the jobs which it is hoped will, by enabling informed choice, ensure commitment to the new roles and structures.

Toshiba – managing rewards

An entirely new approach was taken in designing the reward systems. What was needed were reward systems that supported high quality productive output, flexibly. Where possible, the egalitarian approach considered in other aspects of the organisation's development were considered; in principle, at whatever level everyone should be treated similarly. The principle was adopted therefore of a fundamentally 'single status' system albeit that different levels of pay would apply. There were no job descriptions, which it had been agreed would create rigidity, so there were limitations in scope for a truly evaluated system.

A wholly pragmatic approach was taken to deal with management salaries, each being determined in accordance with what the company could afford related to indicators of market rate. The broad considerations were:

☐ Did it feel right, was the individual happy with it?
☐ Were there to be any likely problems of differential?
☐ Could the company afford it?

More art than science was used, in line with the criteria for the selection of the top team.

For other employees, what was aimed for was a structure that would be fair but not treat everyone as absolutely equal when in truth they were not. A broad-based classification system was used, with the following criteria:

1   Job grading based on:

   ☐ absolute level of skill
   ☐ multiplicity of skills
   ☐ multiplicity of operations with a skill.

2   Sub-sections within a skill:

   ☐ single operation ability
   ☐ multiple operation ability.

3   Degree of skill:

   ☐ single skill ability
   ☐ multiple skill ability.

4   Overall flexibility:

   ☐ multiple skill and operation ability.

From consideration of these criteria, a principle was developed: to reward individual employees on the basis of proficiency over a range of job skills and the flexibility of their contribution to the company.

Four grade definitions were determined based upon the use of this principle. The definitions were:

Grade 1   New employee – general clerical or general assembly. Temporary staff single skill or range of skills but only in one department.

Grade 2   At least three skills with at least one in another department.

Grade 3   The full range of assembly skills across all production departments. Clerical/administrative skills across all administration departments. Subkey operator skills in production, ie at least three operations in addition to Grade 2 skill level.

Grade 4   Key operator skills in production, ie all key operations. Technical support to all assembly operations with recognised craft/technical qualifications. Key operations in administration. Business/commercial qualifications.

There would be no rewards for timekeeping or attendance, these being quality standards to be expected of everyone. Equally, there were to be no bonus arrangements of any kind. Later developments involved experimentation with a company-wide 'dividend' based upon company performance but this was discontinued. There was also, later, admittance of some variations of pay within a grade band based upon overall assessment of performance following an annual assessment, discussed with the employee. This applies to all levels of employee.

The systems adopted had bare-bone simplicity but broadly achieved the objectives that had been wished for. The systems were notably integrated with development activity, so employees were effectively rewarded for developing their skills and for being willing to apply them in whatever way the company needed at a particular time. There were, thereby, degrees of choice; the only limitations being the training opportunities available at any one time. These were generally allocated on a first come first served basis depending upon skill area chosen. Good records are necessary to support this.

The biggest perceived problem, with the particular flat organisational structure that was adopted, was how individuals would be motivated when they had got as far as they could through skill acquisitions. Also, for the supervisors at the lower end of the management tree there would be limited opportunities for progression and hence increase in reward through promotion. Despite these anticipations, the extent of difficulty over the years has not been so great.

The issue of pay has been kept alive through particular responsibility of the company advisory board (COAB) which has stood in place of conventional negotiating structures. A working party of COAB drawn from union and non-union members at all levels has the task of monitoring pay issues through examination of what's happening nationally, locally and in the industry sector of the company, considering then the company's financial standing, and coming forward with all relevant known facts for consideration by the full board. COAB then gives the company appropriate 'advice'. So far, that 'advice' has always been accepted by the company. The concept here is that full and open consideration of all the facts by everyone leads everyone to similar conclusions. The consideration involved and the related debate are not capable of simple description, and encompass the whole range of individual views and feelings; what is key, however, is that these discussions are entirely open with no point having been overlooked – a brave concept, perhaps, but one which so far has worked.

8

MANAGING MORALE AND
MOMENTUM

☐ Morale and momentum need managing.

☐ Communications are critical but simple communications processes, such as 'cascading', cannot be relied upon. Multifaceted communication is required.

☐ Inconsistency of actions and behaviour undermine both morale and momentum.

☐ Speed of action and the extent of involvement are critical.

☐ Ownership of processes and accountability for actions at all levels need to be clear.

☐ Getting people feeling part of something successful is an important remedy.

Maintaining morale and momentum really goes hand in hand with coping with distractions and diversions. They are part of the same continuum, but here they are emphasised as positive actions to build and capitalise upon positive reactions and responses.

Focus and integration

Chapter 1 of this book includes commentary on failed BPR initiatives: of concentration upon technical and operational decisions; their merits and disadvantages; and of paying insufficient attention to the way that people are involved as individuals and groups and how they feel and react; consequently, their needs are not sufficiently taken into account and the process grinds to a halt, goes off in the wrong direction or fades to a degree; of not achieving the original performance vision. These practices are common in Western society and contrast interestingly with the approach taken in Japan. Western practices of concentration on the 'what'; decisiveness in decision taking and the sequence of subsequent actions which then involve people to a greater or lesser extent and to almost certain better effectiveness of the Japanese approach of considering all of the issues at length and widely throughout an organisation before pressing a 'go' button. Japanese implementation happens very fast compared to Western organisations. Nevertheless, while Japanese organisations are notable for holistic thinking, programmes need not necessarily be rolled out only when all of the answers are known. There can be significant overlap between the actions required during the planning stage and the preparation for the implementation stage. In summary, the Western system provides for quick decisions, a longer implementation period, less involvement in both planning and implementation providing more opportunity for resistance and subsequent implementation delays and frustrations. The Japanese approach involves longer consideration and decision making, shorter implementation phase, more involvement in planning and implementation strategies and generally speaking a more supportive implementation process.

Overlaps
Two lessons can be drawn from the Japanese approach without consideration of the wider cultural issues that are undoubtedly involved. These are:

1   Concern for behavioural acceptance supportive to the new ways starting during the planning stages is beneficial.
2   The launching of phased and overlapping projects before all planning and the overall picture is complete is feasible.

Japanese consensus-building processes are alien to Western practices and are unlikely to be easily transferable, certainly to cope in the shorter term with a largely new culture being introduced which might involve more consultative or consensus processes. Therefore, without that benefit, Western organisations need to give extra attention to positive attitude orientation of those involved. The development of some form of cultural map of the organisation as it exists, compared with a notional map of the organisation that might need to exist, needs to be prepared and strategies developed to bridge the gap between the two. Initiatives will need to be taken to minimise worries, enhance understanding and engage positive support. To counteract political resistance, a pro-change grouping or platform needs to be built that is powerful enough to, if necessary, overcome resistance. An overall plan of actions and required resources, needs to be prepared. Planning must be conducted in a way which permits early initiation of pilot projects.

Thus, planning can work on a continuum in concert with implementation, though this is not always appropriate. Bass undertook its top-level planning over a relatively short period and then rolled out interlocking projects. After having 'disbanded' the top planning team their subsequent experience led them to conclude that it would have been better to have maintained this group for much longer to provide co-ordinating focus. In the case of Toshiba, the organisational model was, because of the time constraint needed for rapid implementation, contained in a short period and developed to final organisational model stage. There is, however, no one way.

In order to ensure effective implementation, 'implementability' needs to be taken into account in the planning stages. Planning needs to deal with both problem solving and behavioural issues.

During the planning phases, there needs to be a clear vision of the reasons and objectives of the planning activity. There should be no assumption that all involved in the planning process have requisite skills either to identify all the issues or to undertake appropriate analytical tasks. Specialist support may be appropriate to help those involved.

Management and communications

All managers who will be involved or responsible for implementation need to be involved in the planning of the implementation and, in order to gain their commitment, need an extremely clear vision of what has gone before. Top management nevertheless need to provide a continuing contribution in ensuring organisational acceptance. The vision from top management and how they portray that, is of considerable significance in ensuring success. The methods of communication need to be multistranded. Reliance cannot be given to 'cascading' processes; top management need to communicate directly, in person, and through a whole variety of other channels. The range of possibilities for such channels is very well illustrated in the Bass Taverns case study. Those involved in all of the cases studied are united in their view that it is necessary to communicate, communicate and still more communicate ... but the right information at the right time and the right kind of listening at the right time.

Concurrent with implementation and ongoing planning processes, as a programme is rolled out in phases (if that strategy is adopted) there will be a need to communicate extensively with those who are, perhaps as yet, not affected. In particular 'good news' needs, as one case study writer has suggested, 'to be shouted loudly from the roof tops'. The best kind of news in a change process is good news; good news that what has been implemented has worked and good news that what has been implemented is acceptable or even satisfying to those involved. The engagement of strategically placed 'missionaries' is a very positive move. The more people, particularly in influential positions, that are supporting the initiatives and helping share the good news, the more the activities of cynics and sceptics will be minimised.

Acting quickly and decisively both to maintain momentum and to concentrate any grief, can also be a helpful action. Rolling out the process stage by stage after difficulties have gently been overcome is unlikely to bear the kind of fruit needed in the kind of change brought about by BPR.

Prevent inconsistency

One of the greatest contributors to undermining morale and momentum is inconsistency. Absence of inconsistency will not directly bring about positive support and applause; its absence will probably go unnoticed! Presence of inconsistency that does not bear added good explanation or self-evident rationale, will bring about at least some negative response. Prevention must always be preferable to cure. The investment in finding the route to avoidance of inconsistency may not be easy and, the larger the organisation, the harder it will be to both spot the inconsistencies and to find the best available ways forward.

Clarity and consensus

Clarity of the purpose can be a valuable countervailing mechanism but equally can constrain creative thought and the development of novel solutions. The tensions between the need for devolvement and central co-ordination for the greater good may not be easy but ways must be found. The Japanese consensus-building processes of extensive horizontal, diagonal and vertical involvement (all two-way) until everyone is prepared to endorse acceptance is a powerful, though time-consuming, methodology. It offers reconciliation of devolved activities with top-down co-ordination, but its capability to work is significantly conditioned by the culturally conditioned attitudes and behaviours of Japanese society. The communications processes adopted in Toshiba at Plymouth have few similarities with communications within companies in Japan (Toshiba and otherwise). At Plymouth, a forum of employees from all levels and a wide range of occupations (COAB) exerts considerable influence, though not decision making. It can be argued that the very absence of decision-making capability adds to the power of the influence exerted by the forum. The way that the forum works as part and only part of the processes for resolving operational and other matters should not be lost. While the forum did not exist at the time before implementation of the major change within Toshiba described in this book it has subsequently coped with major organisational issues in a way that suggests that the mechanism might have scope for wider transferability. As a mechanism for at least inhibiting inconsistency it certainly offers something significant.

Transmission and reception

On a further point with regard to communication, the multiple strand approach and the need for repeating and other reinforcements are vital. Clarity of communication can depend upon the way things are presented. Even the following simple sentence might not be immediately understood, particularly if presented in an unfamiliar way:

I know you believe
you understand
what you think I said
but I am not sure
you realise
that what you heard
is not
what I meant.

Communication of a message one way or the other is not complete until the party receiving it understands it in the way that the party sending it intends it to be understood. Repetition and conveying the message in different words using different media and mechanisms will be required. Those receiving 'good news' may infer that the news is not as good as they are being told or may not believe the news at all. Those receiving 'bad' news may not believe the news is as bad as they are being told. The message, particularly when conveyed cross-culturally may not be understood at all. Contrasts of both the context and the content of message giving will provide wide variation for interpretation and misinterpretation. Consistent restating of the message, in both the same and different forms, will reinforce consistent comprehension.

In our society, completeness of messages also aids acceptance and comprehension. Half messages and particularly inferred messages, where explicit content is required for comprehension, should be avoided.

Communications skills

It is no good expecting outstanding communications if those involved don't themselves have the requisite skills to carry it through. Some individuals have outstanding personal skills and sensitivities and such individuals can exert powerful positive influence. It is notable that all of the chief executives in the case studies contained in this book have been acknowledged to have exceptional communications skills. All of the top planning teams have featured at least one individual with a particular responsibility for communication, skilfully exercised. Communication within BPR, like all other BPR elements, needs preparation, planning, top-level commitment and substantial resources of: (a) the right kind, in terms of people, and (b) an adequate amount, in terms of money. Further, the range of mechanisms and media needs to be as wide as possible in line with the issues arising in the particular case and can include some or all of the following:

☐ one-to-one personal communication, one-to-group and vice versa
☐ personal communication, audio, video, telephone and teleconferencing, letter, memo, broad sheet, booklet, and others.

Compensate fairly

Fairly compensating and supporting the practical needs of casualties can be a positive investment for the ongoing organisation. Acceptance of a sense of 'fairness' among the survivors will help generate a positive attitude. Voluntarism can be a double-edged sword as there is also a tendency to lose individuals who the organisation may wish to keep. Support mechanisms can both help individuals and sometimes help the organisation, such as organisation set-up with company help by former IBM employees who were then available to provide specific services required by the organisation, and at the same time could develop a wider customer base beyond their former employer. Given proper attention, costs which might otherwise have been just a drain on organisational resources can cause value to be added to the efforts and attitudes within the ongoing organisation.

Reward survivors

Rewards for survivors in monetary and other forms, according to their contribution can help, but the message that is aimed to be given through such mechanisms, for both the short and the longer term, should be considered. Monetary and other material rewards are no substitute for saying 'thank you', preferably face to face. When people feel that their contribution has been observed and acknowledged, and they feel valued, the contribution can be compounded. The cheapest and most effective motivator is being appreciated.

Bass Taverns – managing morale and momentum

The board's role has been to communicate the overall vision and to make sure via the change champions that the vision is really shared. One of the first things the Bass change team did was to put on a massive nation-wide road show to paint the big picture and also to highlight how change would affect various work groups. We could not rely on normal briefing channels and cascading methodologies to get the change story across. Nor could we rule out malevolent compliance, so we made over twenty presentations nationwide – each one led by a board member.

We utilised all the channels mentioned earlier to get our messages across and we engaged in a continuous debate with the business about the way ahead. We promoted some of our project managers to territory managers, and they became our missionaries in the field. We actively engaged the resistance to change forces head on, and succeeded in 'turning them'. Many of our converts became our most avid supporters.

Essentially, we acted quickly. By concentrating the grief we managed to sustain performance, but our BPR activity in Operations was about building the business and growth and, therefore, we had lots of good news, as well as bad news for the few.

All these activities helped in managing morale but we certainly did not maintain it for the whole of the change process.

The Leicester Royal Infirmary – managing morale and momentum

The goal of The Leicester Royal Infirmary re-engineering programme is nothing less than organisational transformation. The level of upheaval created by such major change and the momentum and energy required to sustain it cannot last indefinitely. The hospital's experience suggests the following:

1   *Do it quickly*. Originally The Leicester Royal Infirmary programme involved the sequential (one by one) re-engineering of the core healthcare teaching and research processes. Six months into the programme a decision was

made to re-engineer all the core processes concurrently. There was such a high degree of interaction between hospital processes that without concurrent re-engineering processes risked being sub-optimised. 'Support' processes could only be re-engineered when the support needs of the core healthcare teaching and research processes were known. If the support processes were re-engineered in advance of the core processes they could deliver the wrong services. Management of a partially re-engineered organisation is challenging, and the time over which this occurs should be minimised. During re-engineering, multiple systems have had to be maintained while the hospital has reorientated itself into a process-driven organisation.

2   *Get many people involved as early as possible.* Early evidence from The Leicester Royal Infirmary programme indicated discontent from those not directly involved in the programme from its inception. For example, there were concerns about professional boundaries from those not involved in the initial skill-enhancement activities.

3   *Communicate widely.* The communication strategy should be both generic with broad messages about the programme *and* highly targeted and focused to meet the communication needs of specific groups. Every group should be covered and the communication medium should reflect specific needs. For instance, at The Leicester Royal Infirmary there was a particular problem in communication with junior doctors who deliver much of the healthcare service yet who don't 'fit' into any of the channels through which normal communication takes place.

4   *Ownership and accountability.* Ensure that line managers and key clinicians are leading and owning the change. Senior managers have a critical role. They must protect the organisation as it reinvents itself. This requires proactive management of the external environment and ensuring that patients continue to receive effective services while re-engineering is going on. The leadership demonstrated by the trust chairman and chief executive is characterised by active involvement, personal demonstration and recognition of individuals' achievements.

Rank Xerox – managing morale and momentum

Maintaining morale while laying off 10 per cent of the Rank Xerox workforce was not easy. But it was achieved during 1994 through several main factors.

Fournier, the managing director, had throughout been very clear and consistent on his intentions. His vision was clear, and he defined the problem, not the solution. The restructuring was based on need, logic and analysis, not on a lawnmower approach of reducing every area by 10 per cent. The early confusion generated by any reorganisation dissolved relatively quickly, because the design had been well thought out and an increasing number of people were involved in planning the implementation. In customer business units, managers and teams were more in control of their business activities and results. There were early wins for the business and the people in 1994 in growing customer satisfaction, revenue and return on assets, towards the desired state. Success breeds success, and the feeling of motivation was tangible in the newly implemented organisations. Despite the layoffs, there was some growth in new areas such as facilities management.

Handling layoffs was still a problem. Rank Xerox had experience with smaller scale reductions, and the evidence in many cases was that the people who left found themselves well equipped, both financially and in experience, to make a good start in other companies. The people who stayed sometimes had more problems; they saw other people leaving, without understanding the reasons for individual departures, and not knowing where the process would end. Uncertainty for the future was the biggest single worry quoted by many people. Even more communication was necessary, and more counselling for the people who stayed would have been helpful.

The evidence for improved motivation was measured in the 1994 Employee Surveys. Since 1990, Rank Xerox has carried out 100 per cent surveys of European employees, comparing country results with the respective national averages. In 1994 the results were also available at work-group level, enabling each team to respond to detailed concerns, with team-based improvement plans. There were areas of difficulty, especially where customer satisfaction was in some cases at risk during

implementation, but in virtually all countries, employee satisfaction improved significantly.

Royal Bank of Scotland – managing morale and momentum

Implementation is the acid test of management, nowhere more
sorely tested than during a large business process re-engineering programme. Perhaps the time has now come for us to think
of IQ not as intelligence quotient but as Implementation
Quotient. However, what percentage of management-led initiatives in large British companies typically get implemented
sufficiently well to impact the performance of the firm?

The collective view of many of those involved in the Columbus Change Programme in the Royal Bank of Scotland was that
implementation quotients (IQs) were invariably below 50 per
cent. From benchmarking visits both in the UK and USA, an
IQ of nearer 25 per cent was more typical. It is hardly surprising therefore that implementation has risen to the top of the
management agenda over the last few years and was, for all
involved in Columbus, a major preoccupation.

'Making it happen' was the way Sir John Harvey-Jones chose
to define the problem in his book of the same title. His solution was leadership: 'Everything I learn teaches me that it is
only when you work *with* rather than against people, that
achievement and lasting success is possible.' However, for
many of the organisations with whom we conducted benchmarking visits, the recurring theme was ownership by the top
teams, for change was often subcontracted to middle
managers, who applied the tried and tested methodology of
management. This invariably meant dutifully measuring,
reporting and controlling. None of these dimensions appear in
descriptions of leadership.

So, can there be a 'theory of implementation', or is theorising about implementation a manifestation of the disease of
which it might claim to be the 'cure'? Isn't implementation the
stage at which all theorising is exhausted and only practice
remains? Shouldn't theory retire hurt at the point that implementation begins?

One approach to this line of argument is to suggest that
when a management team has difficulty 'making it happen',

the problem invariably lies in the 'it' that they want to happen. Both these shortcomings spring from a fundamental theoretical error; in other words, problems of implementation are always a symptom of some earlier error, either in the formulation of the objectives to be realised or the organisational culture. From an HR perspective it was our argument that if it were not for these errors, implementation would be seamless.

What we had to be wary of was the argument, that 'What doesn't get done in business deserves to remain undone'. Having scoured the literature on organisation behaviour and reviewed benchmarking data from other change programmes, it was clear to us that there was already a theory of implementation in the existing literature – what no one had been able to do in our experience was string it all together. Therefore, flawed implementation should always take us back to either the quality of the vision inspiring the change or the quality of the management processes supporting change.

What follows are 10 suggestions for more seamless implementation based on experience in the Royal Bank of Scotland which are framed against Harvey-Jones' observation about success and lasting achievement coming only 'when you work with rather than against people'. Five of the suggestions relate to the kinds of corporate vision that inspire action; the remaining five to the kinds of organisational culture that facilitate change.

It's at times like this one is reminded of the dictum, 'Successful strategy is never copy-cat strategy'. It is always difficult and dangerous to generalise, especially about management and corporate performance, where the art often lies in breaking 'rules' rather than conforming to them. With that proviso in mind, these 10 suggestions or principles are presented as 'characteristics of success' that we have observed.

They have been written deliberately to challenge. Working on the premise that managing change is one of the toughest tasks that human beings can give themselves; that the track record of corporate renewal programmes is abysmal; that British companies are not exactly overwhelmed with management teams skilled in the arts of 'harnessing, motivating and leading people', to use another of Harvey-Jones' most telling phases; and that no excuse is required for arguing that something radical is required to break the log jam.

Visions that inspire ...

1   A vision must be the authentic impression of a single
    person. Most visions fail to inspire because they look like
    the work of a committee. No one in the Royal Bank
    doubted that it was the vision of the Retail Bank manag-
    ing director, Schofield, to 'build the best performing retail
    bank in the UK by 1997'. He was relentless in communi-
    cating and testing the validity of that vision.

2   A vision refreshes the parts that ordinary business objec-
    tives cannot reach. It breaks the traditional rule that
    objectives should be Specific, Measurable, Achievable,
    Realistic and Time related (SMART). A vision can sets
    sights so high that any chance of success requires radical
    new ways of thinking and acting.

3   A vision is a substitute for strategic plans, not a preamble
    to them. It starts from the premise that most of the events
    in the future that will affect the business are impossible to
    forecast and therefore strategic planning is a fraud. The
    strategic plan for the Retail Bank is therefore not a tight
    concise document full of measurement metrics but a series
    of challenging goals that define the vision.

4   A vision lulls the rational manager's mind into raising the
    risk, narrowing the focus and differentiating the output of
    the business to entrepreneurial levels of discomfort. As the
    change programme has rolled out, the vision provides the
    backcloth for the behavioural change necessary to achieve
    sustained success. To paraphrase Sigmund Freud, 'If you
    wish someone to change their behaviour, first get them to
    change their point of view.' Vision, supported by a frame-
    work to take action and led from the top, can do this.

5   A vision makes a business so manageable that it can virtu-
    ally dispense with middle managers. By engaging people
    throughout the organisation in discussion and debate, the
    vision can act as the aiming point with which everyone can
    identify.

Organisation cultures that deliver ...

1   Implementation is, at the root, redesigning the manage-
    ment processes of the business to align them with the

vision. That's the model we endeavoured to follow.

2   Implementation demands first and foremost, an organisation that is structured around the vision – focused upon critical customer-serving processes, not around functions, technologies or geographies. This is sometimes known as the 'horizontal organisation'. Segmenting the Retail Bank to focus on the personal, commercial, business and corporate customer meant that the bank's efforts were designed to address their needs rather than the opposite. This element of implementation took the most time, energy and effort; however, having a clear shared vision ensured that when huge problems reared their head, they were overcome by raising the risk and narrowing the focus.

3   Implementation meant, for us, managers 'letting go', not 'tightening up'; and empowering implementation teams makes them free to discover not constrained to obey.

4   Implementation needs to feel exciting and impactful for those carrying it out. The design of the change programme engaged a huge organisation-wide audience in the research and development phase. As implementation was carried out in geographic markets, the moment the new management teams were appointed they were immediately released to drive the change in their segment of the business. This includes selecting their teams and reframing the vision.

5   Implementation requires the support of a menu of organisational learning resources on a 'just-in-time' not a 'need-to-know' basis. Designing, developing and implementing learning that is focused on the learners' needs rather than the educators', creates its own tensions. However, to secure an implementation quotient greater than 50 per cent, this is where a sizeable investment both in time, energy and resources has to be made. From benchmarking data we recognised that many organisation renewal programmes failed due to an under investment in aligning the learning resources to the change effort.

Maintaining morale during the bank's change programme has much to do with the formulation of the objectives to be realised. However, by being clear about the vision and the principles of implementation, the IQ was raised dramatically.

In our experience at the Royal Bank, individuals' orientation and willingness to take risks and embrace impactful change is directly related to their proximity to it (Figure 8.1). By working hard at sharing the vision, informing our implementation process with insights from both the academic literature on, for example, realistic job previews, models of organisational commitment and stress, together with data from other change programmes, the size of the quadrants could be changed dramatically. Alternatively by thinking about implementation holistically and integrating all interventions to support the vision, the rejection, resistance and denial quadrant can be reduced dramatically.

Figure 8.1

ROYAL BANK OF SCOTLAND'S MATRIX ON RESPONSE TO CHANGE

	Short Term	Long Term
Low (Impact on self)	Enthusiasm remains undimmed	Rampant enthusiasm
High (Impact on self)	Rejection, resistance and denial	Fear, suspicion and public compliance

Toshiba – managing morale and momentum

Toshiba wasn't to have the opportunity of involving lots of people, nor did time-scales permit 'pilot' subprojects. What had been designed was a start when everything would come into place at once. The first day of production under the new arrangements would be for real. Everyone had to be prepared for their new roles, operating in an entirely new way. This would be a big enough task, but there was, in the meantime, another: to maintain production in order to continue to supply Toshiba's customers. Stocks had also to be built up in order to cope with a period between the final shut-down of the joint venture and the opening of the new organisation, albeit a relatively short period. The objectives of setting up something entirely new at the same time as maintaining production were not mutually supportive and each required different strategies though they needed to be considered in concert.

There was unquestionably a need for 'visioning'. Employees needed to be inspired to wish to be part of the new operation, but not to be in any way misled about the likely realities. If individuals were not likely to feel comfortable with the highly disciplined 'clockwork' organisation that was proposed then they should be given sufficient information to decide, on their own account, to self-select out, that is, to withdraw. A video was produced that pulled no punches. It talked about the idealistic operating standards, the kind of commitment that was going to be required of employees and the absolute attention that was going to be needed with regard to detail. Considerable emphasis was put on non-tolerance of absenteeism and the need for flexible working. But it also explained the positive aspects; the new ways of communicating including the creation of an advisory board with its members elected from all parts of the company that would 'advise the company on conditions, on future prospects, and on anything the members feel they have advice to offer about'. Mention was made of the unqualified support that the union was giving.

Firing up enthusiasm for the new organisation was important but it also had to be finely timed. If information was presented too early, interest could wane. If decisions were taken too soon on selection, those who wanted to join but for one reason or another could not be accepted would be particularly disheartened and hardly motivated over a long period of time to maintain their commitment to supporting current output. Timing of release of information and making of decisions was finely balanced.

Every applicant at whatever level was required to view the recruitment video and also another video that was produced which explained in more detail the workings of the advisory board and the company's interface with the union. This jointly featured the managing director and a national officer of the union.

Whether or not employees were going to become part of the new enterprise, the manufacture of televisions had to continue. Incentives to continue to work included scope for making an application for the new enterprise and a monetary bonus for all who continued to the end of the joint venture. In any event, all (including those who would be joining the new organisation) would receive redundancy compensation. Timing of the final redundancy notices was also critical. Production was maintained but the nearer the date came to final closure of the joint venture the more difficult it was to maintain standards and quality of work from some of those who would not be continuing. Plans for early release in some cases were brought into effect.

Many employees were not motivated to join the new business; only about a third actually pursued applications, choosing to take up other opportunities. A few set up their own businesses, some to supply the new company. Indeed, a number of employees with particular skills that the new company would have definitely liked to utilise decided not to join. In one sense at least the company strategy to strike a balance and be absolutely truthful paid off; there was not an overwhelming move to apply, there being roughly three applicants for each job. A balance, it was felt, had been struck.

Those selected for the new operation had, in part, to undergo training beyond their normal working hours with the joint venture company. But most training was done in the two or three weeks immediately prior to opening. Certain supervisory staff and others were sent to Japan to view how a 'clockwork' factory might work. But the numbers sent were not great. The most difficult area to train for and perhaps the one that was least successfully done was training for supervisors and managers to inculcate the new behaviours required of them. This wasn't a disaster but they didn't easily fit into their new roles and it took time for them to let go of the old roles, styles and attitudes.

By far the biggest impact was the 'big-bang' type of start-up when, on the first day, all systems, all processes, all policies started and the company aimed to produce a given realistic quantity to a given quality standard. The standard of 'right first time' products was achieved, as was the quantity. What the company had termed as 'shock treatment' for its start-off operations did work. People were shocked into doing what they had undertaken to do and they were mostly delighted. The start-up process created a real bond among those taking part and everyone shared in a sense of achievement when what had been planned was shown actually to work. From the start there was consistency of operation. Deviations of any sort from the plan other than adaptions which were communally agreed were nipped in the bud. Some found the going not to their liking and chose to leave but after about three months things settled down. The quantity and quality of output steadily increased. Absenteeism levels of around 12 per cent in normal terms for the joint venture company were cut by more than two-thirds, and employee timekeeping became near perfect. Through technology, systems (including greater outsourcing) and work efficiency, a threefold increase in productivity was almost immediately achieved.

Attention to people issues within the organisation was carried through to suppliers. These were considered an extension of the company. Their attitudes and work practices would have to be changed as much as those directly employed, and programmes and resources were applied towards this end.

Within the company, a sustaining and encouraging influence was undoubtedly actually feeling part of something successful. The influence of fairly widespread favourable press coverage probably also played its part in helping to bind employees together. Indeed, on one press visit when a reporter asked to talk with a spokesperson he was offered the opportunity to talk to anyone he liked in the factory; an endorsement of the trust that had been inculcated but also, itself, a powerful statement by the company of the level of responsibility that it was expecting from every employee.

9

MANAGING THE AFTERMATH

- ☐ The 'aftermath' is as much part of re-engineering as implementation.
- ☐ Managing the aftermath requires multidimensional information.
- ☐ Stress management is fundamental.
- ☐ Reward management and human resource planning have to be done well.
- ☐ Good news needs reinforcing with celebration.
- ☐ Communications, as in other things, is vital; maintaining communications processes requires structured discipline.
- ☐ A learning culture supports flexible work processes.
- ☐ Major step-change like BPR needs to be followed by continuing change in smaller steps.

Each case study organisation's experiences are different but they all agree that managing the aftermath is as much part of BPR as planning, designing and implementing. If not properly managed, what has been achieved will regress. Former or otherwise undesired behaviours will emerge.

Sequential stages of teambuilding have been distinctively and succinctly described as Forming, Storming, Norming and Performing. BPR has similar phases, though the Storming generally precedes the Forming. BPR Norming and Performing are inextricably linked and together encompass what can be described as 'the aftermath'. The Leicester Royal Infirmary case study describes the aftermath phase as 'embedding'. The aftermath *should* be the state in which an organisation finds itself after a successful re-engineering process, but too many organisations 'count their chickens before they're hatched'. For the purposes of this chapter, therefore, we will consider the aftermath as being any time after launch of implementation. One message that comes over loud and clear from all of the case study organisations, is that the people aspects of implementation and beyond are much, much more complex than ever they imagined.

The range of issues

The importance of information

Managing anything requires information. Managing an aftermath is no exception. Without knowing what is going on through 'taking the temperature', as with bodily fever, it is necessary to monitor progress on a regular basis; to watch the trends and take appropriate action. As with the monitoring of a human body after a major operation, taking the temperature is, alone, not enough. A Business Process Re-engineering process is an operation of immense scale. Widespread and multifaceted monitoring is therefore required, at the individual, work group and organisation-wide levels.

For the component parts and the whole to be seen to be working together, a range of measures is first required, from which interpretations can be made towards understanding what is going on. While the productive 'outputs' are perhaps the most important measures, without monitoring the contributing processes it will not be possible to spot or anticipate difficulties and thence take corrective action. Monitoring, in order to see the trends, requires recording and plotting on an ongoing basis. Without this, difficulties (and solutions) will not become visible. These will be needed for the benefit not only of the change in view but for initiatives that will, perhaps, follow, at another time or even in another place. Managing the aftermath therefore is not something that just starts after implementation. The preparation phase of managing the aftermath needs to start early in BPR activity.

Managing stress

Major change will always increase the levels of stress in an organisation. The causes may not be able to be eliminated (like having to work much harder and longer during the change, and the level of insecurity induced by fear of loss or change of job). It is nevertheless open for organisations to ensure that these causes are not compounded by incidental causes, such as:

☐ erratic management style
☐ poor communication
☐ overwork, particularly among managers
☐ lack of opportunity to influence the way work is carried out.

Management of stress becomes a very important element of managing change, and is fundamental to the management of the aftermath. Stress levels will almost certainly be one of the elements which will require anticipating, monitoring and acting upon if negative and counterproductive behaviours are to be minimised. There is a useful guide.[41]

Managing rewards in their widest sense, including pay, career paths and other positive reinforcement processes, is an essential part of managing the aftermath (see Chapter 7). Unanticipated issues will emerge even in the best managed situations.

Creating impetus
Where a 'clean break' situation of the whole organisation can be utilised, as in the Toshiba case, where change was implemented at the same time throughout the company (so-called 'shock treatment'), continuity of the new processes can more easily be reinforced, as everyone is 'in the same boat'. The Leicester Royal Infirmary, however, has to ensure the maintenance of clinical standards on an ongoing basis. This kind of situation brings added complexity and requires more time and resources to, as they have said, 'sort things out'. The key is the establishment and constant communication of the required service levels. The withdrawal of extra staff that might have been required to facilitate change has to be planned, otherwise their roles, which are only temporary, will become embedded.

The danger of complacency
In all situations, complacency is the greatest enemy of managing the aftermath. To assume that just because everything seems to be working, that is not to say that it will stay that way, or that the

judgement is correct. Constant focus on the desired outcomes (behavioural and performance), expressed both as positive outcomes and reduction or absence of negative outcomes (such as complaints or queries), will be necessary. Earlier behaviours and ways of doing things probably took decades to evolve. Embedding new ones cannot happen instantaneously. It's rather like teaching someone a new language; they'll be enthused and excited about being able to communicate in their new-found tongue and may seek every opportunity to use it. But in their lower moments and when they are tired or otherwise seeking relaxation, they will seek to revert to their mother tongue. Reversion will more likely come when for some reason things have not been going right. Reinforcement will be required but, it is suggested, not by allowing a brief respite of temporary reversion. Like the 'just one' cigarette or drink for those who are notionally trying to give them up, such reversions will most likely ensure they don't. Kicking old habits can be a painful process. What is needed is positive reinforcement of the beneficial outcomes, to individuals, the team and the organisation.

Exploit the limelight

Exploiting and extending what is known as the Hawthorn effect[42] can help. Bringing the spotlight on employees through overt internal interest of, say, the chief executive, or external interest, as from the media, can work very effectively, though remember that the media will not be under control and may focus on certain issues in an unhelpful way. Nevertheless, true co-operation and involvement with the press can itself inhibit difficulties; given greater access there is less need for them to embroider or to surmise.

Research and measurement

Measurement and benchmarking will allow what seemed like extraordinarily ambitious targets to look, at certain stages, quite capable of being exceeded, such as in the case of Rank Xerox. At Rank Xerox, the effort required to lift the return on assets from 7 per cent to 18 per cent has shown the viability of achieving even better returns without the need for further fundamental change. Choice of the 'right' measures is obviously important. Professional help rather than gifted amateur design and analysis will pay benefits. Royal Bank of Scotland's investment in using independent psychologists to review certain aspects led to identification of new opportunities for improvement that would probably not have been identified in other ways, and certainly not in time-scales that actually enabled action to be taken within and for the benefit of the programme. We apologise to those readers who would like us to provide a list of things that should be monitored. What should be monitored and in what way will depend upon the circumstances. We do not advocate any one set of measures. The actual processes that determine what measures might be needed are the substance of success. The consideration given to that is part of the design process; it is the starting point. Single suitable solutions will not be found in textbooks.

Celebrate

Telling the 'good news' is important but is not enough. Achievements need *celebrating*. The social interaction combined with visible awards (see Chapter 7) will reinforce communication through enjoyment. Mistakes also need to be made visible and, if dealt with in an open and fun way, can become positive reinforcers rather than negative ones. When Toshiba's managing director was the first one to breach a new no smoking rule, *he* went out of his way to admit it and tell people what he had done; he gained tremendous respect in the process. The process of publicising the no smoking rule could not have been better supported, to the delight of many and the pain of no one. That was a spontaneous opportunity but a planned practice could be to celebrate admitted mistakes (to celebrate the opportunity for them not to be repeated). When anyone speaks negatively, as distinct from constructively critical thoughts, a gong could be sounded and demerit points recorded on a wall chart; those having greater demerits being required to undertake a penalty, like buying the first round of drinks at the next social event. Planned and carried out in concert, communication of successes and failures can together help build better behaviour.

Multiple communications channels

The more channels of communication, the better. Good and bad news communicated by recently battle-scarred heroes acting as ambassadors of the new revolution will hold great sway. Emphasis needs to be put on the word *recent*; tales from the trenches may be interesting to listen to but stories quickly lose freshness and can become boring. The range of communication initiatives within Bass Taverns was exemplary. The Leicester Royal Infirmary shared with other cases the allocation of someone with a dedicated role to manage communications. If it is important, then resources, including management resources, are required. Bass selected a consummate professional communicator for the role. The Leicester Royal Infirmary initially chose a nurse with requisite skills and undoubted connections. The choice was undoubtedly as strategic as it was sensitive.

Discipline

If communication is the keystone, then discipline is the mortar that holds it and everything else in place. It is no good deciding upon a particular course of action if it is allowed gradually to fall into disuse. How many company policies are allowed merely to fade away? If those policies required considerable thought and involvement to put them in place, they should require similar consideration to dispense or replace them. If meetings are arranged for a particular group to deal with a particular topic, it does nothing for consistency if some (and especially top management) don't show up and others drift in some time after the meeting has started. This is not an avocation for regimentation; just an emphasis of the point that it is more the behaviours of those involved that will condition the outcomes than the 'rules' themselves. This becomes ever more important during the aftermath phase, when new personalities may appear, especially at the top. Changes in leadership need to be made consistent with the behaviours successfully recently induced. In the Toshiba case, the most challenging recruitment and selection job ever undertaken by those involved was to find a replacement managing director to take the organisation forward, one who was of the highest calibre but who would not be tempted to 'dig up' the recently laid foundations.

The population of the wider work group will be probably anything but static. Over time, through people moving round or leaving, the original team focus and spirit, helped by shared difficulties and the excitement of participating in something new, will tend to become dissipated. The kind of 'discipline' mentioned above might help hold people's bodies but it won't wholly hold their minds.

Group skills and time horizons
Reforming actions need to continue to be taken at the group level. Selection of new entrants assumes critical new dimensions. New attitudes and skills will probably be needed. The mechanisms for first identifying and then ensuring these standards are critical. It can't be afforded for them to be undertaken sloppily. New entrants are the seed corn of the continuum and of further change. Flexibility of mind and openness of attitude are important. Trainability to required behaviours as much as inherent skills are important. Trainability in rapidly changing circumstances is of considerable value. Long-termism is not necessarily the order of the day, but neither is reactive short-termism. Perhaps the 20th century will herald the age of medium-termism. Indeed, through greater meeting of minds between East (long-term thinking) and the West (relatively short-term thinking), there seems to be movement toward the centre ground.

Keeping going
If total quality management (TQM) was what an organisation 'did' before the huge step-change of business process re-engineering, then that is also what it should be doing after BPR. Continuous improvements (often now referred to in the West by use of the Japanese word 'Kaizen'), with continuing smaller incremental step-changes, and inherent attention to collective quality needs and attitudes, is undoubtedly appropriate. The authors see no conflict between TQM and BPR but see them as complementary processes.

The importance of learning
Training in considerable measure will always be required to bring about learning of new technologies, new processes and new skills. Processes that require precision teamwork will also

require training interventions to help embed seamless team-working. Without appropriate and timely training in these domains, effective re-engineering will not be achieved. Just-in-time learning of this kind will be both more productive and more cost-effective. Nevertheless, the authors wish to emphasise a more important aspect of learning in the workplace that goes beyond the generally accepted context of the word training. It arises from the subtlety of the point that, with humans, one does not generally provide instruction to bring about voluntary adult behaviour. That is not to say that indoctrination methods will not work; just that regimented application of what people have come to characterise as training/instruction are not so appropriate for the kinds of voluntary behaviours needed to be brought about and maintained. Constant reinforcement has a kinship with indoctrination but embedding automatons is not what today's re-engineered organisations should be about if they want to avoid ossification.

The conditions for learning

Leaner, fitter and more flexible workforces demand flexible, sensitive, creative and empowering methodologies to help bring about learning. 'Fun' can be a powerful feature in the positive reinforcement of learning. Accountability of line managers for, and their direct involvement in learning, through counselling and coaching, are much more the order of the day. Facilitation of the development of staff is widely considered the most important of managerial responsibilities in Japan. Surveys indicate that more than 20 per cent of Japanese managers' and supervisors' time is allocated to training-related tasks.[43] Western managers certainly have something to learn from Japan in that respect. The most important condition for successful learning in the workplace is a positive attitude towards learning among all those involved. Organisations whose policies and practices recognise this need and which set about the means to stimulate more positive attitudes will be providing for themselves the bedrock of future flexibility and growth.

Management of continuous learning and development is at the heart of managing the aftermath.

Bass Taverns – managing the aftermath

Responsiveness on the part of managerial survivors is the key to successful implementation of change: responsiveness in relation to new team requirements; responsiveness in relation to creative and innovative suggestions coming from the new teams; responsiveness in relation to cries for help as well as cries for additional resources.

It is about embracing a customer philosophy and changing behaviour towards satisfying customer needs and then the inward and almost incestuous orientation of survivors is rapidly changed to one of an outward orientation and delighting customers.

The inevitable and necessary feeling of guilt felt by survivors towards casualties, which is reinforced by the 'ceremonies of departure', is then quickly superseded by one of relief. It is then that the new goals and objectives have to become real in the minds of the men and women who form the teams in the core processes.

The goal is movement towards a *development* ideology for the company in all its main and subsystems (Figure 9.1). We are not arguing the case for 'throwing the baby out with the bath-water' but we need to measure how we are progressing along these lines in order to facilitate the management of the aftermath. With major change, we feel that the period of grief needs to be short: the period of change everlasting.

Figure 9.1

TOWARDS A DEVELOPMENTAL IDEOLOGY

From		To
Control	→	Development
Individual orientation	→	Team orientation
Short term	→	Long-term growth
'Safety'	→	Risk-taking
Job for life	→	Performance-related

The Leicester Royal Infirmary – managing the aftermath

A consistent theme from re-engineering experiences across the sectors is the sheer effort involved in implementing re-engineered processes. Our experience from a hospital perspective is that implementation is followed by a further stage entitled 'embedding' which is equally challenging.

A diagnostic testing centre for patients was an outstanding success at pilot stage. Multiskilled patient testers were able to undertake a range of tests, patients had to undress only once and results were available within 40 minutes. However, in order to secure the centre's ongoing operation, many issues had to be resolved over a time-scale of several months. Job roles had to be formally agreed and recruitment and training programmes undertaken for both full-time patient testers and staff who would provide cover. The management arrangements were not straightforward. It was decided that a 'user' department should be responsible for the operation of the centre on a day-to-day basis as an interim measure. This separated the process management from the responsibility for ensuring clinical standards were met. Service level agreements had to be established. This 'embedding' process took many hundreds of managerial and clinical hours to sort out. There were no shortcuts.

Re-engineering was widely communicated within The Leicester Royal Infirmary as offering dramatic improvement in critical measures of performance. This raised the expectations of some staff that the performance would improve as soon as implementation took place. Our experience showed that it can take several months for new skills and working relationships to be assimilated. Performance may temporarily drop before it improves.

Some ex-supervisors have continued in the system in the short term to act as 'facilitators' in the change to new working roles. One lesson learnt is that the withdrawal of such roles should be clearly programmed. Otherwise, a pattern of reliance and 'permanent fixture' status may ensue.

The training and development agenda at The Leicester Royal Infirmary is enormous. Such activities have worked best when co-ordinated at organisation-wide level to ensure consistency and organisation-wide coverage. However, ownership, involvement and accountability have to be with local managers.

Patient expectations continually rise. When the 'norm' is a three-hour service rather than a three-week service, the challenge is to provide it even more effectively or with even better patient outcomes.

A major aim of the re-engineering programme is to create a culture of adaptability and wholesale organisational learning. Staff across the hospital are becoming equipped to challenge existing practice, seek solutions to problems and to implement. If the re-engineered organisation does not continue to challenge and reinvent itself, the programme will not have succeeded.

Rank Xerox – managing the aftermath

The Rank Xerox implementation is still in progress. Full achievement of the new design was planned to take three years, and the supporting processes for people development, skills training, technology and systems need continuous investment and support. There could be a risk of loss of momentum over this period, but the evidence so far is of strong support for full implementation. Two reasons are likely.

1   The operational business is increasingly the responsibility of the customer business units, so support managers in HQ groups can pay attention to the development of all the necessary supporting infrastructure.

2   The CBUs themselves form a very demanding and powerful group in specifying and implementing new processes. They react quickly to customer pressures, and are impatient with any delays in providing support. In many cases they develop improvements which can be extended to other units. Across the company, there is a better balance between staff and operational pressures.

The company has also begun to realise that 18 per cent return on assets need not be a ceiling on performance. Achieving 18 per cent looked difficult enough, but the benchmarking showed it was possible without fundamental change in processes. Radical improvements in process and skills could yield yet higher returns, market leadership and more security for employees in an increasingly competitive market-place. The search for improvement has begun well but, like total quality, truly effective process management may always be on the horizon.

For many years Rank Xerox had been a very stable organisation, with little turnover in middle management levels. There is now recognition that while there is still an important place for experience, growth and change will increasingly be driven by younger managers, and a policy to achieve a better balance of age, background and diversity is being implemented. The role of staff support groups is still developing. There are still operational tasks in HRM which are performed by HR specialists, which should be transferred to line managers and teams. The HQ groups need to become more strategic, defining what is possible, and reduce further in staff and costs while improving in change and project management. Non-core activities are being outsourced – in the supply chain, information management, general building services, Rank Xerox has entered into partnerships with long-term strategic suppliers of these services.

Royal Bank of Scotland – managing the aftermath

Someone once said the only three things you have to remember about buying a property are: location, location and location. The same could be said about change programmes where the three most important things are communication, communication and communication.

Realising that the communication process was going to be critical to the outcome of the change programme, a dedicated communications business initiative team was created within the Columbus programme. Benchmarking research had told us than many technically sound change programmes had been undermined by employee resistance. It was managing director Schofield's desire to minimise the risk of this happening, by insisting that any communication process had to adopt the frame of reference of those to whom we were communicating. A fundamental message that had to be ingrained on the psyche of the Retail Bank was the concept that change was going to be ever present.

The design and presentation of *New Roles in a New Bank*, which included the principles and commitments for the 'employee proposition' of rewards, careers, development and selection, was the beginning of 'norming' the new culture and reinforcing the scale of changes to come. No longer were there to be generalised careers, but focused careers designed around specialisation. For these to work, the career paths, rewards education and development process had to be made explicit. Furthermore, by flattening the organisation considerably, we had to bear in mind how people could develop and build careers horizontally within a specialism and provide a map showing where the bridges were into other areas of specialisation. This ensured that although the fundamental structures were changing, the scope to grow and develop would not diminish. However, in designing the new career process it was imperative, in breaking up the old organisation, not to build another that was equally obsolete.

A major test of the HR processes was when, in March 1994, the decision was taken to implement all elements of the core business process redesign in Glasgow. Employing nearly 1,200 people and accounting for a significant proportion of the Retail Bank's business, Glasgow was to be a major test of both the process design and the 'stomach' of the organisation to follow through its design intentions.

Other regions have gained considerably from the lessons learnt in Glasgow, which was no comfort for the staff involved. While regular Columbus updates had been given, videos made, briefings held, few pay real attention to the impact of change until it is imminent (see Figure 8.1 on page 176). The first shock, in spite of the publicity and discussions surrounding the launch of *New Roles in a New Bank*, was when managers were invited to apply for one of the new roles described in the brochure. This was further compounded by inviting them to attend competency-based interviews. In most cases, in spite of 15–20+ year careers with the bank, few had ever attended a job interview! The selection process sent shock waves of seismic proportions throughout the organisation. Not only did it become the guardian of the programme's integrity but also it introduced a new cultural framework, based around people discussing actual performance and achievements.

The selection process provides an example of how learning in the Glasgow phase of the change programme was applied subsequently. One of the young HR officers, seeking a final project for her IPD Graduateship, was asked to conduct a review of how people felt about the selection process. This research gave some useful insights that informed on how the process was modified for application elsewhere. One result of this being that a more explicit description of the process was written, to include worked examples of application form completion and typical questions that might be asked at interviews.

Early on in the Columbus programme a framework for continuous organisational learning was established through the process redesign model (see Figure 5.1 on page 115). Using selection as an example, once Glasgow was implemented, a more rigorous review took place that included a full-scale audit of the whole selection process conducted by independent occupational psychologists, Pearn Kandola. They also identified opportunities for improvement and, more to the point, provided a stiff examination that ensured the HR team did not become complacent once the first phase of implementation had ended. Subsequent phases of the roll-out have been heavily influenced by our experience in Glasgow. This includes holding 'job fairs' in advance of the changes being implemented. At these job fairs, holders of the new jobs are available to discuss their jobs, revised copies of *New Roles in a New Bank* are available, video examples of typical interviews are shown and booklets describing the whole process in some detail are given to all staff. Together this gives reassurance and creates the basis for providing the most explicit realistic job preview possible. The programme is enhanced, because it is communicated largely by those who have already gone through the process. In doing so, both the positive elements, ie 'the process is fair', and the less positive, 'it was hard and demanding', are put into the public domain. In the past there would have been little or no discussion.

The continuous review process and the need to regularly report to the change management group has facilitated learning through the Socratic process of discussion and needing to explain each critical step. The learning process has been further enhanced by each new phase of the programme being implemented by a fresh management team, all of whom have a different perspective from their colleagues. In many cases, this dialogue ensures the programme continues to gain strength from being based around a vision. As each new management team is put in place, their implementation of the vision, as they see it, ceases to be cast in tablets of stone, ensuring it becomes dynamic.

Perhaps the biggest challenge for all staff, but particularly those who provide leadership, has been to make the fundamental changes in a highly competitive environment. This requires them to embrace change and learn from others abandoning the 'not invented here' syndrome. This can so easily emerge when creating new legions of 'Jedi knights' who, having successfully navigated the arduous selection process, have irrepressible belief in their own ability. Their belief can also be an Achilles' heel, as many can lose sight of the value of learning from others.

Toshiba – managing the aftermath

Having brought about the new organisation, got everyone in place and commenced operations, there was soon realisation that the company was at the *beginning* of something rather than at the end. While targets were being achieved there were all manner of teething problems, though nothing fundamental. At least the basic design concept proved to be sound; in particular, the communication processes put in place provided a vehicle for difficulties to be raised and resolutions to be found. Without these having first been firmly embedded there is some doubt whether the framework would have held. They have undoubtedly helped the establishment of the bedrock of trust on which all other management processes have been sustained. Absolute adherence to the communications and consultation processes, as well as the open style of management demanded, supported the 'norming' of the new culture. All had been involved in the previous joint venture and most felt that the new ways were much to be preferred. Most, that is, but not all; some found the disciplines uncomfortable, that empowerment brought obligations and responsibility. These few left within the first few months. For the remainder, it was a time for continuous review and individual adjustment.

Growth in the demand for product and for highest quality standards kept everyone focused. During the early months a number of Japanese advisers had been employed in the production areas. Their tenacious pursuit of excellence and the involving way that they treated employees on the shop floor earned them considerable respect, though their persistence sometimes irritated. When it was time for them to return to Japan there was consternation among some employees who felt that without the influence of the Japanese, pretty soon supervision would revert to type. That concern was to be, to an extent, well founded. Remedial measures had to be taken, with pressure from both above and below. It wasn't resistance as such, just a feeling that it was easier to do things the way they knew more directly, rather than involving people. Earlier investment in more attitude and skills training of supervisors would have paid dividends.

Entirely new skills were required. The demands of management and requirements for those involved in the company advisory board (COAB) were such that levels of financial knowledge and understanding had to be developed. The decision to train shop stewards and supervisors together was a positive one, taken to help build further bridges of personal as well as technical understanding.

Keeping everyone informed of what was going on, in every dimension, at the section, department and company levels, occupied a lot of effort and investment. Videos were made after every COAB meeting as a quick and consistent means of communication. Subsequently, these were supplemented by briefing meetings to department managers. The video recordings as well as notes from the meetings form a permanent record of exploration in discussion and outcome.

Benchmarking, which had not been part of the original preparation process, came into play to provide comparison of the new company's performance against other Toshiba production units. When quality levels reached those achieved in Japan there was a cause for celebration.

It had been anticipated that the 'flatter' organisation offering limited promotion opportunities would be a problem;

indeed, the academic who had reviewed the organisational plans had identified this in particular. In the event, major difficulties did not arise. Growth in the business undoubtedly helped. Within five years the business had grown nearly fourfold. Those that had been part of the original joint venture were now outnumbered by newcomers. Six years on from start-up it was decided to undertake a comprehensive review and employee attitude surveys. A very high response (82 per cent) was achieved. By and large, the results provided an endorsement of the company's processes but there were critical observations. Feedback that favouritism was a leading reason for 'getting on' brought about a careful review of advancement procedures. Relationships with superiors were good but there was certainly room for improvement. There was endorsement of the general style and the aim to be an open company was positively indicated, and 70 per cent felt that the company advisory board was either effective, very effective or extremely effective. There was found to be room for improvement in the way that management and union worked together in the interests of members. In overall terms the survey aimed to evaluate how the workforce saw the new systems and the new overall approach that had been brought in. The results varied between those who had experienced the previous joint venture company and its predecessors, and younger and newer employees, some of whom had not previously worked, who were not in any position to compare. One thing that the survey could not mask was that making televisions is a pretty boring business and despite the flexibility afforded there was not much chance of getting on. Certainly, the excitement of participating in something new was by now long gone. Nevertheless, the survey gave a lot of comfort that the organisation was still in good shape by comparison with other organisations. The open styles which include openness to criticism admitted particular areas of improvement, which were then addressed.

While the main processes designed from the outset have remained in place, largely unchanged, there has been progress and change on many matters of detail and introduction of new processes of substance. From the outset of the new organisation there was no attempt to introduce quality circles. There had been *ad hoc* small circle activity where groups of employees came together to solve particular problems but not much beyond that. Significantly, through employee initiative rather than management imposition (though with encouragement), quality circles have developed and now become part of the culture, thus further emphasising the participative processes in place within the organisation.

The organisation has responded to many challenges and dealt with many difficulties. In one year, more than 52 new models of television were introduced which put a considerable strain upon personnel at all levels. The organisation expanded, opening another factory to manufacture microwave ovens, the volatile market-place determining that this be closed some years later. That part of the organisation now profitably manufactures air-conditioning products. From early and difficult beginnings, television manufacture has grown such that Toshiba colour televisions products have progressed from about fifth place in the market, measured by volume sales, to first. The competitivity of the market-place provides a constant source of challenge and pressure. While job security was one of the things in the job survey recognised as one of the most valued aspects of employment with Toshiba, no one now believes that security can be guaranteed. Nevertheless, Toshiba is viewed as a successful and mainly stable organisation. Despite changes in people and products its main organisational principles remain in force, much as designed. That is not to say that they will not have a limited life span, but at least the mechanisms admit and have, so far, coped adequately with major change.

10

UNIVERSAL LESSONS AND ESSENTIAL POSTSCRIPTS

☐ Business process re-engineering is an integrated process.
☐ People are essential 're-engineering components'. Managing *with* people's feelings is an important part of managing operations processes.
☐ The abilities, personal qualities and co-operative contributions of people are the elements that ensure re-engineering success.
☐ The principal people barriers are inadequate leadership, insufficient communication, inappropriate structures, inadequate preparation and misaligned systems.
☐ Overcoming the barriers is the required prime point of focus for attention and effort. Resources and thoughtful planning are required.
☐ The impact of BPR upon human resources systems and processes is profound. In re-engineered organisations, human resource management will never be the same again.

The insights of all the contributors to this book are gathered together in this chapter. The contributions are distillations of what has been learnt, often through having made mistakes. Business process re-engineering cannot be undertaken without prospects of slipping or stumbling. What is offered here, by formerly bruised and in some cases permanently scarred expeditionaries, are not prescriptions but the essence of their combined experiences for the benefit of those who come after or those who wish to compare their experiences and conclusions with others.

New horizons

All involved have gone beyond the boundaries of hitherto conventional wisdom; been caused to step outside the box; and have ventured into the unknown. The Royal Bank of Scotland's Columbus project could not have been more aptly named. That, like the other case studies in this book, started as a journey with no certain destination, except for a vision and/or a mission. Centuries ago, Christopher Columbus set out for the Far East by sailing west and found a way to the 'New World'. He came back with stories and with evidence of great riches to be found, as well as the first navigation charts, enabling others to get there. Today, the journey, by different means and routes, is routine for thousands of people every day.

The 'navigation charts' that we can offer, like the first ones brought back by Christopher Columbus' expedition, do not provide certain routes but they do identify the general direction, the major hazards that are likely to be encountered and where those hazards broadly lie. For those who don't prepare for the BPR voyage or flight, and don't keep alert to the perils that are now known to exist and other more particular ones yet to be come across, the prospects of 'foundering' or 'crashing' are extremely high. Knowing the kind of provisions that will be required for the journey, the qualities needed of the crew, what kind of look-out to mount and, significantly, the general skills required of the master or pilot, the risks can undoubtedly be reduced. These, and the selection of the 'vessel' (the means of undertaking the BPR journey) and its suitability and readiness, are the issues falling under *risk identification*, first mentioned in Chapter 2. The actual journey, and its return, with an updated chart for the benefit of other travellers, is that part falling under the requirements of *risk management*.

Using the framework outlined in Chapter 1, we will review the elements to identifying the risks, barriers and means to resolution. The issues are not standalone elements but each interfaces and interacts with the others, as illustrated in

Figure 10.1

INTERACTION AND INTEGRATION

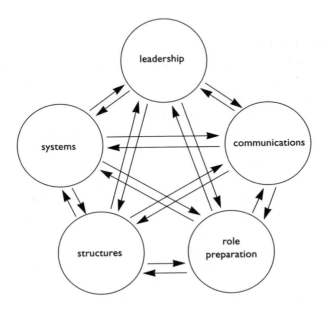

Figure 10.1. Consideration of the barriers to integration of each of these elements, necessary for organisational synergy and successful re-engineering, are used to draw out the universal lessons.

Barriers to successful synergy

Inadequate leadership
Inadequate leadership is the first and fundamental barrier to re-engineered change. Virtually every study of re-engineering and all of the cases illustrated in this book have acknowledged the importance of leadership. This is necessary at every level but is especially critical at the CEO level.

Beyond other requisite business skills and knowledge, there are at least twelve personal qualities, capabilities and commitments that are required of CEOs at the head of a re-engineering programme. In no special order, these are listed in Table 10.1.

Table 10.1

PERSONAL QUALITIES, CAPABILITIES AND COMMITMENTS REQUIRED OF RE-ENGINEERING CEOS

Personal qualities, capabilities and commitment	Rationale
Open-mindedness	Not to be constrained by what has gone before. To be prepared to recognise the need to discard principles and practices hitherto held dear.
Courage	To be able to throw away things they've had a hand in creating and, perhaps, to say good-bye to old friends and allies.
Risk-taking	To accept the risks, but with application of skill to reduce the odds of losing and improve the chances of winning. In order to assess risks, identification of them is first required.
Vision	To have for himself or herself an unswerving view of what needs to be achieved, in business terms.
Communications capability	Bringing about change, as distinct from just setting and demanding standards, requires a different kind of communications capability. Charisma may be helpful but not all effective drivers of change are charismatic. Charisma can be compensated for in other ways, not the least of which is evident resolve.
Visibility	Bringing about change can be significantly facilitated by the visibility of the overall leader. 'Walking the talk' is a phrase sometimes used. Presence of the leader in all places and within all levels provides important reinforcement.
Consensus-building capability	Re-engineering requires the tenacious pursuit of getting everyone willingly agreeing or accepting where they are going. This requires listening more than promoting.
Delegating the delivery	Means 'hands-off' management rather than 'hands on'; to acquire the best possible 'field commanders' and, after direction, being able to let them get on with it. Conditions for success may be provided from the command centre but success is won in the field. Delivery relates to planning, design and implementation. Delegation does not mean abrogation of their accountability.
Consistency	Pursuit of the ideals and goals, including compatibility of personal actions that don't give conflicting messages.
Significant time	To give to all stages. If 20 per cent of time is committed in the early stages (which many would see as minimum) then 50 per cent may be required as the process rolls forward into implementation. And it does not stop there; commitment of time to reinforce the managing of the aftermath and the continuum beyond is vital.
Resource provision	The CEO has an important job, to ensure that the very best people are made available, cutting across any political pressures and divides. Also, to ensure that the back-up resources are made available at the planning, design, implementation and aftermath stages. Time and money are required.
Sense of urgency	To induce and maintain impetus, which is vital for re-engineering work.

Table 10.2

NEW ROLES FOR HIGH INVOLVEMENT LEADERS

Role	Role description
Delegator	Moves decision making to lower job levels; sees that responsibility and authority accompany job tasks.
Visionary	Visualises a more perfect future; expresses potential achievements of the work unit consistent with the organisation's vision.
Change agent	Looks for better ways to perform work by challenging current paradigms and encouraging improvement ideas from direct reports and external stakeholders.
Inspirer	Communicates the vision and inspires acceptance of and commitment to it.
Model (trust)	Personally illustrates priorities and values, is both trusting and trustworthy.
Coach	Helps others learn to be self-sufficient through personal development and arranging learning environments.
Teambuilder	Establishes and supports teams that engage in self-managing activities.
Supporter	Constantly expresses confidence in direct reports' self-sufficiency and treats their mistakes as learning opportunities.
Champion	Visibly celebrates accomplishments of direct reports; promotes their best ideas to higher management.
Facilitator	Provides resources (materials, information, etc.) for the work group; removes obstacles that impede the group's progress.
Partner	Builds alliances with and communication bridges to other work units and external partners.

The personal qualities for CEOs given in Table 10.1 are demanding, integrated, requirements; they are not standalone elements. They are very much interrelated, so that communications, visibility and time become part of one action. They are, however, each an essential ingredient. Many of them require the generation of trust. Charles Handy and Gerald Andrews emphasise the criticality of trust within empowerment programmes. In a recipe for success, lack of the smallest ingredient can make all the difference, especially face-to-face contact. Handy says: 'Visionary leaders, no matter how articulate, are not enough. A shared commitment still requires personal contact to make it real ... High Tech has to be balanced by High Touch to build High Trust organisations.'[44]

Andrews emphasises the extent to which mistrust by leaders and/or participants in empowerment and quality programmes undermines the capability for success.[45] Trust is the adhesive required to hold all the leadership building blocks together.

The study by Howard and Wellins, referred to in Chapter 1 on page 8, identified specific new roles for those involved at all levels of leadership within high-involvement programmes (Table 10.2).[46]

Whatever new organisational and job structures evolve during a re-engineering programme, there is no doubt that the requirement for leadership in all its forms is enhanced rather than reduced. Wilson, George and Wellins identify the realities of moves towards empowered teams within organisations which have parallels with much of what goes on within re-engineering, summarised in Table 10.3.[47]

Table 10.3

NEW REALITIES OF LEADERSHIP

1	*Teams always need good leaders* – it's the nature of leadership that changes.
2	*Leaders gain power in the transition to teams* – from enabling process improvements, attracting resources, removing barriers, making things happen outside the team, helping team members realise their potential.
3	*Most leaders are capable of making the transition successfully* – 20 per cent will survive whatever, 20 per cent won't make it, 60 per cent will make the transformation if given help.
4	*New leaders must be direct* – they need to loosen reins, not drop them, move from giving directions to providing direction.
5	*Leaders need to relax – it's OK to make mistakes* – admitting and learning from mistakes will earn leaders respect faster than any other type of behaviour.

All these issues bring challenges for those involved in transforming an organisation. Managers who have spent much of their career 'controlling' subordinates will not find the new glove an easy fit. New skills and attitudes have to be developed. This highlights the need for training and support at all levels. Given that, the realities are promising.

Insufficient communication
Insufficient communication is the second barrier to successful

business process re-engineering. Communicating the compelling case for change is the overriding task. It has been stated repeatedly in this book that you cannot communicate too much; that is true, so long as what is to be communicated is appropriate and the timing is right. Getting the volume, content and manner of communication right are the challenges to be faced. Communication at the wrong time (both too early and too late) can be as useless as no communication at all. Just-in-time communications are what are required. The link between the organisation's corporate strategy and its people is the initial bridge that has to be built; this requires multidirectional communication which involves significant listening, again at the right time.

Most people will assert that communication is important. Regrettably, few of them can describe what they mean by good communication, or even intelligently describe the process of communication beyond a few methods of communicating. Dave Francis usefully breaks down the processes of communication into four main segments, showing *purposes* for communications, with each of these segments shown to have three constituent supporting elements:[48]

1   Communications for sharing the vision or mission

   □ persuasive management
   □ compelling vision
   □ sensitivity to the external environment.

2   Communications for integrating effort

   □ integrating mechanisms
   □ helpful geography, eg workplace layout
   □ downward flow.

3   Communications for making intelligent decisions

   □ communications skills
   □ apt administration
   □ upward flow.

4   Communications for sustaining a 'healthy' community

   □ high trust
   □ lack of prejudice

☐ supportive behaviour.

For each of the four segments and each of the supporting elements there are equal and opposite forces which can be described as 'blockages to communication'. So, with regard to making intelligent decisions, the blockages would be: (a) *inadequate* communications skills, where individuals do not have eg appropriate listening skills, (b) *inept* administration, where information may be passed but may not be recorded or made available to those who neeed it, and (c) *defective* upward flow where the mechanisms are either not in place or are not used. Such models are useful to organisations who wish to think intelligently about their own systems of communications. Against each 'blockage' a structured assessment can be made and appropriate countervailing actions taken.

As an example, drawn from the case of Toshiba, some of the facilitating actions to support 'integrating effort' were:

☐ A provision for formal and informal communications at various levels, ie daily five-minute section meetings, monthly department meetings, monthly advisory board meetings, etc.
☐ Emphasis on the *total* system.
☐ Explicit expression of an 'open' system.
☐ Published framework procedures.
☐ Immediate feedback on work performance (individual and group) and its effect on the whole.
☐ Common workwear for everyone.
☐ Open-plan workspace for everyone.
☐ Visibility and accessibility of managers and directors.
☐ Small circle activity.
☐ A requirement that the communication systems in place will work, eg obligatory attendance; no deferred meetings.
☐ Notice boards in work sections, managed by employees.
☐ Logical workplace layouts.
☐ Production managers' workspace and meeting space on the shop floor.
☐ Open circulation of minutes/notes within strict timetables.
☐ Structured and participative report-back meetings.

☐ Use of video for consistency of some messages.

☐ Single-status facilities and terms of employment.

☐ Half-yearly plenary meetings.

It should be noticed from those examples, that the *mechanisms* underpinning communication are as much a feature as the *processes*.

Here is a checklist of issues that have been observed that support communications effort:

1 Actions speak louder than words. Make sure what you *do* matches what you *say*.

2 Attitude surveys are important tools but they need professional design and careful company preparation.

3 Be consistent; don't keep 'adjusting' the message.

4 Communicate especially well to team leaders/managers.

5 Communicate facts, especially relative facts.

6 Communicate performance.

7 Communicate quality in terms that are meaningful (external and internal comparisons).

8 Communicating with technology helps provide speed and consistency but it is not a substitute for face to face.

9 Develop the skills of those who show promise.

10 Don't communicate promises you want to keep, only promises you can and will keep.

11 Don't communicate what you don't know.

12 Don't rely upon 'trickle-down' processes.

13 Invest in improving manager and team leader presentation skills.

14 Involving people aids communication.

15 It's not easy to make silk purses out of sows' ears: select the best communicators.

16 Listen to feelings; seek to understand those feelings.

17 Listen to the customers; involve the customers.

18 Make a record of what you listen to.

19 Make communication part of everyday work life.

20 Multifaceted communication works best.

21 Newspaper communication does not change behaviour.
22 No one believes they are a poor communicator; feedback is necessary.
23 Presentation by people who are not committed can be counter-productive.
24 Presentation by people who don't understand is useless; improve understanding.
25 Provide ways and means for everyone to communicate better.
26 Research attitudes, and continue to measure them.
27 Seek facts.
28 Tell only the truth; the truth will always emerge eventually.
29 Timing is as important as the message.
30 Translate values into specifics before communicating.
31 Use all the senses.
32 Use 'converts' as missionaries.
33 Use pictures to reinforce words.
34 Use written information sparingly; always prepare it carefully.
35 Wherever possible, communicate directly (face to face).

Appropriate and timely communication
While you can't communicate enough in the 'right' way, *what* and *when* something is communicated can be critical. The scenarios in Table 10.4 need to be avoided.

The key essential to communicate in re-engineering
Above everything else, communicate the organisational/business reasons *why* any change is necessary. At the same time, communicate what the alternatives to no change are. Without first gaining acceptance of the need for change, there will be no short- or medium-term opportunity to introduce or embed change effectively.

Inappropriate structures
Organisation structures which have developed in tandem with specifically defined job roles and hierarchies do not provide the

Table 10.4

THE WRONG 'RIGHT' COMMUNICATION

	Example	Possible solutions
The right information given or received *at the wrong time*	Information needed for 'design', received during implementation	*Early representational involvement*
	Announcement of a change with no consequences yet available	*Don't make announcements until the whole picture is known*
	When there is no time to consider what is communicated (information given or received), or resources to back it up	*Plan and provide time and resources*
The right information given or received *in the wrong way*	Recipients hearing what they surmise and not what is being said	*Repetition, multiple means of delivery. Ensure skills of corporate deliverers and listeners. Make time available*
	'Bad' news' or 'good' news received impersonally	*Choice of appropriate means. Selection and training of personal communicators*
	Presented by someone not fully understanding or 'committed', or without requisite skills	*Only use 'converts' as communicators. Ensure they have the facts. Ensure they have the right skills*
	Issues affecting feelings communicated in 'unfeeling' ways, eg only by memo	*Choose the means to match the need: People for feelings, paper or technology for facts (usually both)*

framework to support flexible working, constant changes in production or service specification. Manufacturing units earlier designed for long runs of the same goods, restaurants serving one type of customer, service organisations only backing up one type of product or customer, bank branches only dealing with lenders and borrowers and hospitals hitherto serving the bureaucracy as much as the patient, are now all in the process of change. Somewhat fixed structures, built around functional silos with multiple hierarchies competing for attention and power, and with individuals and groups trading information as if it were an internal commodity, are now, through successful re-engineering, in decline. With business process re-engineering, the need is for dramatic change in the way work is undertaken. Such change cannot be sustained without a change to the structures that support the processes. And it is now that way round; not jobs or roles supporting the structure.

Flatter structures with fewer functional and other hierarchies, jobs designed or organised flexibly around business processes, and the emergence of team-based activities, different in kind from earlier concepts of teams, are the main structural changes within re-engineered organisations.

The emergence of different kinds of job roles and the way these interact in a team sense in supporting business processes are the driving forces on structure. No longer is it standard practice to first define the top hierarchy and then cascade the organisational tree on the basis of reporting relationships, dividing up perceived tasks, in line with the scientific methods of Frederick Taylor. Re-engineered, organisation designs emerge more from the bottom up, but in line with higher level needs for appropriate control and co-ordination. Control and co-ordination will be effected in quite different ways than hitherto.

There are some important words of warning on the subject of top-down organisational design. The following quotation, sets the scene:

> We trained hard – but every time we were beginning to form up into teams we would be re-organised. I was to learn later in life that we tend to meet any new situation by reorganising, and a wonderful method it can be for creating the illusion of progress while producing confusion, inefficiency and demoralisation.

The way the business is structured needs to flow from, or at least take into particular account the structure and needs of the teams; not the other way round. The writings from which the quotation was taken, incidentally, were by Petronius, in the 1st century AD. Some ways of doing things truly transcend time!

This book does not attempt to cover any processes for developing an organisational design; only to assert that if your business processes change, then your organisational design will need to change. The way an organisation needs to be structured will depend significantly upon the way people in that organisation need to be able to work in order to support the business processes which serve external and internal customers.

The way that jobs are organised will depend upon the nature of the business. Competencies used flexibly, rather than fixed tasks, become a greater feature. Customer needs become the key focus. Teamworking and greater team and individual autonomy become more common. Outsourcing, with inputs being made from 'outside' resources, is another trend and one where integration with the 'internal' members is often badly managed. In such interfaces, to engage seamless co-operation with quality of input, is extremely important. Overall, most would agree that, managed well, re-engineering can produce jobs that are more challenging and more satisfying.

Of course, 'tasks' have to be performed and it is through 'process mapping', not through collecting tasks together, which comprises the early and fundamental part of BPR activity. Process mapping, with its essential customer focus, comprises identifying the required outputs and requisite inputs, concentrating upon the goals rather than the actions or means. Processes will cross a number of hitherto prescribed functional or organisational 'boundaries'. The greater the range of representation at the analysis stage, the better will be identification of the real processes, as those involved understand more about them than anyone else. With involvement and greater comprehension through participation, the better will people understand the emerging new roles. Processes are the building blocks of BPR; without them business process re-engineering is not possible. They will always show that new 'ways' are required in order to perform them. The nature of work will change. Without response to the emerging new job needs, these essential elements of an organisation's structure will be inappropriately aligned. With re-engineering, the nature of most jobs change. The means to determine the new framework for work and the requirements for people involved, requires careful management, probably with external support.

Newly re-engineered processes do not, in fact, throw up discrete job roles, they throw up discrete processes that require support from *groups* of people. Operating within a re-engineered organisation is essentially a team-based activity. Bringing about cross-functional team-based activities, mainly of a self-directed nature, in an organisation formerly structured more around individuals operating in functional boxes under top-down direction, is one of the great challenges of BPR. Within a re-engineered organisation, a team is usually a 'self-directed team'; an intact group of employees who are responsible for a 'whole' work process or segment, that delivers a product or service to an internal or external customer.[49] They will typically have authority over their work, with individuals within the team, and the team collectively, being empowered to make judgements and take actions without prior agreement of anyone outside the team. They are typically also engaged in and accountable for the processes of continuing improvement. Clearly, such new ways of doing things will contribute to the nature of the organisation. Reporting and control mechanisms will need to be quite different.

Within teams, the nature of teamworking will often be quite different from conventional models. The traditional leader, surrounded by team members looking for direction from him or her, will move towards more egalitarian approaches, perhaps starting with more involvement of the members in decision making, towards a situation where team leadership is a role that moves between members at different times or on different occasions; even to the situation where teams have no defined leader but truly share in all matters. Sometimes, team leadership will be external to the team, with the 'leader' acting more as the team's outside representative, in cross-organisational and resource acquisition activities. The creation of 'virtual teams' is a possibility, particularly in relation to particular projects, with members contributing, with perhaps equal weight, despite considerable disparity between functional capability and status.

In the design of the new structures, it is vital that the 'social' issues, the human aspirations and interfaces of individuals and groups, are taken into account, as much as the technical aspects. These include the roles, the role-holders' need to network, and the desire to provide an environment conducive to the 'spontaneous co-operation' that Elton Mayo so many years ago pioneeringly saw as the ultimate achievement from effective work organisation.[50]

Without integration of all of the means (the operational aspects, leadership, communications, control and co-ordination aspects) there will be disharmony within the structure. The structure and the processes have to be compatible for both holistic working and heuristic development. Change the processes and the structure will need to change. Without changing the structure, the 'old' order of things and its behaviours will tend to be reasserted, undermining the newer, required activities and attitudes.

Inadequate preparation for new roles

New roles will inevitably emerge from re-engineering activity. Assuming that there is clarity of the required 'outputs', these 'clear' definitions are of no use unless they are met. Achieving the required outputs will depend significantly upon:

(a) selection of people with the qualities to be best able to perform the roles; that is, their basic makeup; and

(b) preparation of those people for their 'new' roles.

Just putting people into a new role, to an extent conditions the way they will behave. For example, when a person newly joins an established organisation, they will tend to adapt to the ways of that organisation, but the speed of adaptation will still be dependent upon the appropriateness of their selection in the first place and the induction they are given. Given appropriate selection for an organisation with a strong and clear 'culture' (the 'way we do things round here') people will more rapidly 'conform'. As an example, one of the authors involved in selecting graduate trainees was sometimes faced with a reaction from a manager along the lines of 'I think this person has the right qualities for us but his/her (manner of dress/hairstyle, etc.) puts me off.' Wagering that, if the individual was engaged, he or she would, within three months, conform to the norms of the company without any required intervention, the author never once lost a bet! With no exception, the individuals about whom there had been any concern 'adjusted' to the norms of the group they joined. This, of course, cannot always be the means to achieving required change. In particular, in a situation of change there are, initially, no 'norms'. These have to be aimed for in terms of required behaviours. Required behaviours cannot be achieved by chance.

In a situation where there is not a strong and established way of doing things, people will tend to revert to type and behave in the ways they have been used to. They will be more strongly conditioned by whatever have been their experiences beforehand; with which, through familiarity, they feel more comfortable. Selection (that is, 'preparation' on behalf of the organisation) of people with the right attributes, certainly particular skills and knowledge but, more importantly, the right 'attitudes' are required. On this matter, W. Clement Stone has said:

> There is little difference in people, but that difference makes a
> big difference.
> That little difference is attitude.
> The big difference is whether it is positive or negative.

The positive attitude required in a situation of change includes a predisposition to:

☐ think openly
☐ work flexibly
☐ learn new ways.

The extent to which the 'raw materials' (the people selected) match these qualities will condition the 'preparability' of the workforce. Having all, not just most, of the workforce with a 'positive' attitude is the ultimate aim. 51 per cent of the workforce with a positive attitude will mean that 49 per cent have either a negative or less than positive attitude. The options are rather simplistically but nevertheless importantly illustrated in Figure 10.2. The objective, therefore, is (a) through appropriate selection to get as many as possible willing, or preferably eager, to head more or less in the same direction and (b) to then bring everyone, *willingly* into line, in the 'right' direction. The more who have an appropriate predisposition, the less difficult the process will be.

While selection may start and end with considerations of 'attitude', there is much more work to be done related to defin-

Figure 10.2

THE EFFECT OF DIFFERING ATTITUDES

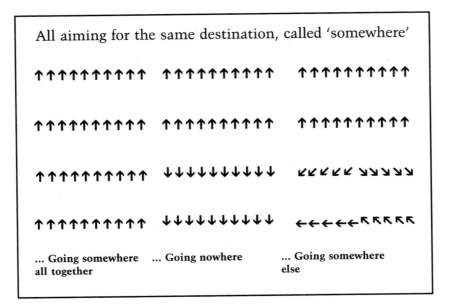

... Going somewhere   ... Going nowhere   ... Going somewhere
all together   else

ing roles and accountabilities and the requisite skills and motivations that will be required for them to be performed
successfully. Role analysis (subtly different from job analysis,
by virtue of more expression of the required outputs and related
inputs, wider than fixed job elements) may lead more directly
to a 'person specification' than going through the hitherto
conventional route of first preparing a job description (totally
devoid in Toshiba). Selection criteria can, as in the case of the
Royal Bank of Scotland, be usefully supported by psychological
research. Whatever, selection criteria needs most careful
consideration and the means of selection needs to be carefully
designed to support application of the criteria which have been
put in place.

If the criteria are very clear, self-selection can be a very powerful tool. The Royal Bank of Scotland and Toshiba, through use
of videos and other supportive material, were open and very
explicit about what they were looking for. Individuals, from that
material and subsequent discussion, were able to exercise their

own judgement and in many cases decided 'That is not for me.' As part of their ongoing selection methodology, Marks & Spencer use forms of self-assessment built into application documentation that enable individuals to 'self-select out'.

One mistake that organisations can make is in 'over-selecting', where qualifications and 'experience' are over specified. Strategic 'under-selection' of perceived requirements is one model worth consideration, where selected individuals fall short in some dimensions of the optimum but, more positively, their capability to learn and grow in a job is high. One fairly new psychometric tool, the 'DNLA' (Discovery of Latent Natural Attributes) specifically aims to address this. Such tools as this and other psychometric tools, used responsibly in conjunction with other means, can prove very useful. Room to grow in a job may be valuable but, for some jobs, selection of perhaps older workers who may have no aspirations for advancement but still have an interest in learning, may provide an exceptionally reliable and stable resource with which to balance knowledge and experience with new ways. The ultimate element of the selection process is what we call 'fitability'. That is, the extent to which individuals 'fit', on a personal level, with the team and the team leader (howsoever called). Final decision by the team leader, preferably with other members of the team, is optimal. If they are to be accountable through empowerment to exercise operational judgements, involvement in choosing their key means (their colleagues) can assume considerable importance. This can even, in some circumstances, extend to selection of the team leader by its members. That is ultimate accountability. Selection goes hand in hand with training and other preparation. Selection provides the base materials on which to build.

Following selection, and before 'commencement', the nature of individual and team role preparation will need to span new technical and process capabilities required and new behaviours needed for optimum performance, in relation to both internal and external interfaces. Technical needs will be organisation specific and will not therefore be much addressed here, but they must be addressed by organisations. Multiskilling in technical and other matters is often both a defined requirement and a natural outcome of re-engineering. Behavioural training needs are, however, the least obvious and perhaps the most important. To achieve required outputs, most preparation will need to be related to the achievement of required behaviours. Behavioural preparations, with different emphasises for different individuals and categories, might typically cover:

- attuning as a group, together, in the new roles, ie 'shaking-down' or getting used to each other
- communication and consensus making
- counselling skills, particularly for leaders
- evaluating and managing individual and team performance
- generating a sense of 'fun'
- handling conflict
- influencing others
- leadership and autonomy
- 'listening' sensitivities and skills
- managing meetings
- one-to-one communication
- peer group and '360 degree' monitoring and feedback
- valuing diversity.

Non-behavioural capabilities that are to a much greater extent required in a re-engineered organisation, include:

- instructional skills
- presentation capabilities
- managing time
- selection skills
- understanding and using quality tools and concepts
- understanding financial and 'budget' information and processes
- undertaking work flow or process analysis
- using idea generation and problem-solving processes and 'tools'.

Role-dependent skills and sensitivities might include:

- concepts and operation of just-in-time (JIT) methods

☐ health and safety, including stress management (and self-management).

The priority and sequence of training needs to be considered on a JIT learning basis. Except for safety or another special reason, it is of lesser priority to learn about something which will not be used at all or for a long time, unless it is to understand the context. On-the-job and off-the-job learning opportunities need co-ordinating. This can be as much a team, as a so-called 'management' issue.

Teams do not happen just because people are thrown together and called a team. Teams, as well as being process tools in any organisation, are social groups of real people, with complex interactions. Team integration and mutual trust is required. 'Virtual teams' that may arise, will need transorganisational trust. Reducing or eliminating all internal counterproductive effort and behaviour will contribute significantly to a healthy organisation, particularly elimination of any internal sense of 'them and us'. Making 'us' a seamless integration of people within the organisation and 'them' only the competition outside is the ideal to be achieved.

Conditions conducive to changing and learning, and resources to support them are required to train and otherwise adequately prepare individuals and teams in ways of behaving that are probably quite different from earlier experience. The conditions need to be consciously and carefully prepared. The required resources (time, people and money) will almost always be extensive.

Earlier in this section, on page 212, we indicated that putting people into a new role conditions the way they will behave, but we cautioned that a strong 'culture' was needed to shape and maintain that behaviour. With major change, however, you can give all the training you can think of, without it having the best effect. There comes a point when you have to create the conditions to 'let go' of old ways, totally embrace the new and just do it. The 'shock treatment' at Toshiba did that ... more change by revolution than evolution; forcing rather than just encouraging change and indicating, in no uncertain terms, that there is no way back. It is at that kind of point that the preparation will pay off. No preparation, and there's no chance. Leave it too late and people will believe that it's not going to happen. The timing of 'go' is a matter of judgement. However, 'go' is only the beginning of a stage which really has no end; maintaining the momentum and managing the aftermath then come into their own...

Misaligned systems

This section contains some fundamental 'crunch points' for human resource practitioners. Chapter 1 (page 12) highlighted the part universally needed to be played by three systems critical to reducing barriers to the delivery of successful re-engineering; redesigned selection systems, redesigned performance management systems and redesigned rewards systems. There are, however, two other universal truths: that (a) these three are not mutually exclusive; other human resource related systems may need to change to meet the particular circumstances of an organisation's delivery of re-engineered operating and information management processes, and (b) that wider changes are required to ensure ongoing organisational success. Along with and including those required for successful implementation of BPR, there are five groups of HR systems:

1   *People resourcing systems*, including role definition, resource planning, selection, performance management and release from the organisation.

2   *Reward systems*, including non-monetary as well as monetary rewards.

3   *Training and development systems*, including suitable conditions for learning.

4   *Employee relations systems*, including individual and collective communications systems and collective representation systems.

5   *Management of HR functions systems*, including team integration, organisational performance monitoring, management of the human resource functions.

These, again, are not mutually exclusive; each to an extent, being interdependent with the others. If there was no integration of HR systems before re-engineering, there should certainly be such integration afterwards.

In a book of this type it is only possible to touch upon the key issues and we will do so by brief examples, indicating in Tables 10.5 to 10.9, by type of system, why there is a need for change and with an indication of some interdependencies.

Table 10.5

RESOURCING SYSTEMS CHANGES

llustrative systems	Indicative reasons why changes to systems are needed	Indicative system interdependencies
Job analysis and job definition	Move from 'role inputs' to 'outputs' and competencies-type focus.	Selection, training and development, team integration, reward, employee relations
Recruitment	Move towards more flexible use of resources; core (permanent), secondary (temporary/part time), outworkers (subcontractors, agency, consultants)	Human resource planning, selection, team integration, performance management, reward
Human resource planning	Change of business and HR strategy, greater flexibility, changed structures, flatter organisation, different career expectations and patterns	Recruitment, selection, training and development, employee relations
Selection	Different job roles, different required skills knowledge and attitudes, more flexibility, changed accountabilities for selection decisions, use of different tools	Human resource planning, recruitment, training and development, employee relations
Employment contract, explicit and implicit	Changes in the 'psychological contract', changes in roles, changes in reporting structures, changes in reward mechanisms	All
Release from the organisation	Change through required ongoing and step-'releases' of resources and the impact on those that stay	Human resource planning, training and development, employee relations, reward

Table 10.6

REWARD SYSTEMS CHANGES

Illustrative systems	Indicative reasons why changes to systems are needed	Indicative system interdependencies
Monetary rewards generally	Changes to individual and team organisation and motivation leading to more team rewards, different roles and responsibilities, devolvement from central controls, focus on process outputs, methods of evaluation and comparison, different career patterns and expectations; need for 'tailored' choice	Role definition. performance management, human resource planning, recruitment, selection, training and development, team integration; employee relations
Non-monetary rewards generally	Changes to leadership styles and processes, individual and team roles and responsibilities, changes in performance management mechanisms; greater willingness to respond to needs for personal recognition	Individual and group communications, performance management; employee relations
Rewards for encouraging new behaviour	Removal of 'old' systems designed for different motivations; emergence of new patterns of work requiring different behaviours; opportunity to respond to emerging wishes for greater individual choice	Human resource planning, recruitment, selection, training and development; employee relations
Rewards for reinforcing required behaviours	New forms of required behaviour; need for new positive and negative reinforcements; opportunity to respond to emerging wishes for greater individual choice	Human resource planning, recruitment, selection, training and development; employee relations
Deferred payment rewards, such as pensions	Different career patterns, shorter employment terms, multiple employments, self-employment; opportunity to respond to emerging wishes for greater individual choice	Human resource planning, training and development; employee relations

Table 10.7

TRAINING AND DEVELOPMENT SYSTEMS CHANGES

Illustrative systems	Indicative reasons why changes to systems are needed	Indicative system interdependencies
Identifiying general training needs	Change in business processes and tools; greater emphasis on strategic rather than individual needs; changes in performance standards; different people to do the identifying; perhaps absence of job descriptions; external as well as internal resources to be trained; changed performance management systems; change from job- to role- and competency-based analysis; increased emphasis on interpersonal skills	Role definition, human resource planning, selection, performance management and reward systems
Identifying individual learning needs	Greater emphasis on strategic business requirements but individual learning needs and learning styles; different people to do the identifying, eg line managers and team leaders, as well as greater individual ownership	Leadership, training and development, selection, performance management
Technological learning	Discontinuous and rapid changes in technology and the learning needs arising; increasing needs for training and retraining; greater goal-oriented conscious influence on development, ie education	Identification of training needs, human resource planning, selection, performance management
Learning related to processes	Greater involvement of individuals and teams in the design of processes and their subsequent evolution	Leadership learning, behavioural learning, technological learning, needs identification, performance management
Behavioural learning (individual and team)	Greater emphasis at all levels on learning new sensitivities and skills related to interpersonal behaviour, ie socialisation and external focus on appropriate customer-oriented behaviour; particular skills and sensitivities to be able to deliver; effective use of external specialists	Technological learning, performance management learning, management of resources
Conditions for learning	Greater emphasis on generation of the psychological conditions for learning	Leadership, management development, team orientation.
Delivery of learning	Changed means of systematic instruction aimed at conscious goal-directed learning, particularly coaching by leaders and peers; greater on-the-job (OTJ) learning delivery	Leadership, selection, human resource planning, performance management
Development generally	Emphasis on the processes and conditions for individuals to achieve fullest potential and emergence of greater self-accountability for this	Leadership, selection, human resource planning, performance management, learning conditions
Management development	Different career patterns, wider definition of 'management', new required skills, knowledge and attitudes; moves from roles based on troubleshooting, volume, conformity and authority, towards enterprise, delegation, management of change, leadership, coaching and initiative	Human resource planning, recruitment, selection, performance management, employee relations
Training for leadership	Acknowledgement of greater communications skills (speaking, facilitating and listening) required of leaders; acceptance of coaching and training roles of managers and supervisors, new means of delegation and control; more decentralised 'ownership' of performance management	Human resource planning, recruitment, selection, performance management, management development

Table 10.8

EMPLOYEE RELATIONS SYSTEMS CHANGES

Illustrative systems	Indicative reasons why changes to systems are needed	Indicative system interdependencies
Collective representation	Decollectivisation of approaches by employers.[51] Changed attitudes and 'agendas' of unions, changed social and political roles of unions	Job design, human resource planning, recruitment, selection, rewards, collective co-operation, communications, release
Collective co-operation, involvement and participation	Emergence of new required ways of involving employees, feelings of loss of prominence by managers[52]	Management development, behavioural learning, process learning, communications
Communications between individuals	Changed channels of communications for sharing organisational vision, integrating effort, making intelligent decisions and sustaining a 'healthy' organisational community	Management development, behavioural learning, team integration, collective co-operation
Pay determination	Moves from nationally negotiated to locally determined; collective towards individual choice and contracts	Reward, management development, communications

Table 10.9

MANAGEMENT OF HR FUNCTION(S) SYSTEMS CHANGES

Illustrative systems	Indicative reasons why changes to systems are needed	Indicative system interdependencies
Benchmarking	Possibly didn't do benchmarking, need for internal, competitive and sector comparators	Potentially all
Performance Management*	Changed vision, critical success factors, roles and responsibilities, relationships, means of formal and informal communication and social interaction; systems suitable for 'local' and even individual needs, rather than standardised and imposed, top-down	Leadership, communications, social, integration, team interaction, reward, benchmarking, employee relations
Team integration	Changed leadership and participation roles, changes in the psychological contract of employment	Management development, selection, training and development, reward
Functional support	Moves towards more developed HRM processes; provision of professional functional support rather than functional delivery	Monitoring, performance management, training and development, human resource planning, recruitment, selection, employee relations

*Included here for convenience; it forms part of most HR and management systems

Bass Taverns – essential postscripts

In any project, essentials can be observed for making things happen. The following are offered from our experience:

1   *Maintain the faith* that what we set out to achieve was achievable. Be prepared to enter the dark night and unknown paths of the innovator. It is a long, lonely, hard road and you do need a good network of sympathetic professional colleagues.

2   *Remove the props.* If there is no alternative to making it happen, eg if you remove the old paperwork-based system then your new IT-based system will work – it has to! You can have parallel runs but only for a short time. If the only way the business or individuals can get investment approved or a budget agreed or expenses paid is via your new systems just watch how quickly staff will learn to operate them.

3   *Benchmark* – not just against the best in your industry, but the best in the world.

4   *People and measures.* Clearly you have to measure as you go in terms of key performance indicators but devote as much of your measurement resources to cultural dimensions and attitudinal climate. Good people and good systems make great organisations; both have to work in concert.

5   *Sustainability* – the trait most required in change champions.

6   *Expect and allow for errors* – and learn from them. Taking risks is about accepting the potential for not always achieving goals. It is the climate created that minimises the potential for errors but at the same time do not deal too harshly with shortfalls. If you make mistakes try and make them cheaply. Cheap prototyping is a source of real advantage.

We made errors, lots of them. Here are some of the things we learned and would now do differently:

☐   *Keep personnel longer.* One of the mistakes we regretted was letting the group of 12 'wise men' or key executives disperse and go back to their business roles. We appointed new team leaders to head up the change projects. This was a grievous error as it took another eight weeks or so to get them 'up to speed' on BPR. Each one of the 12 wise men should have had a facilitating and sponsorship role for a change project.

☐ *More communication and less communication.* We would have devoted even more resources to the communication plan and implementation than we did, but we were undoubtedly guilty of listening too hard and long to the forces of doubt. Instead of bashing our heads against brick walls we should have jumped over or walked round them.

☐ *Avoid any significant dilutions.* We had the appropriate organisation structures devised to deliver our core processes. We allowed the power of the professional functional chimneys to dilute what was a fairly pure organisational form. Even in process-driven organisations, functional power is never dead. Careers remain powerful incentives to sustain relationships with professional hierarchies.

☐ *Implementation.* What makes a strategy truly excellent is implementation and if we have learned but one thing, that is that if you devote £1m to the first phase of your BPR initiative, ie the analysis of core processes; the redesign element of core processes; the laboratory place; the pilots and field trials, etc., then you should devote £10m to the implementation stage in terms of training, education, cultural shifts, attitudinal alignment, etc. It seems obvious but you cannot divorce your strategy from your organisation's core competence. To attempt to do so, results in implementation failure and always will.

The Leicester Royal Infirmary – essential postscripts

The following conclusions were drawn from an evaluation of 'lessons learnt to date' involving key organisational managers, clinical leaders and re-engineering programme leaders.

Essentials for making it happen

☐ Understand the re-engineering roller-coaster – re-engineering consists of enormous highs and lows. Train and equip re-engineering teams to accept this.

- ☐ Learn to anticipate where the 'moments of truth' are likely to occur and anticipate them.
- ☐ Understand that re-engineering is a journey of faith. You have to let go of the shore you are leaving before you can see the shore on the other side.
- ☐ Understand that re-engineering success is 75 per cent sociopolitical and cultural and only 25 per cent rationality and analysis.
- ☐ Make sure that the 'desirable' solution designed by the re-engineering teams appears sensible, justified and worthwhile to the rest of the organisation.
- ☐ While the pace of change must be fast, the need to plan and the need for reflection must be built into the time-scale.
- ☐ Communication must be broad based (across/down/up) and it must be early in the process. The transition of ownership for re-engineering processes must be planned.
- ☐ Re-engineering targets must be stretching, fair and easily understood.
- ☐ Demonstrate the benefits as early as possible.

What would now be done differently?

- ☐ Much earlier involvement of key implementors in the early stages of the re-engineering programme is essential.
- ☐ Understand how difficult and challenging implementation is, and allocate more resources earlier in the re-engineering process.
- ☐ You can never do enough communicating.

Rank Xerox – essential postscripts

At the corporate level Rank Xerox succeeded due to the essentials of a clear vision, the leadership that generated it, and a well thought out rationale for the new design. At the customer business unit (CBU) level, people respond to new powers to support their own business and customers.

Process redesign involved the people who operate the process – be they managers or front-line people. This change was initially an exercise affecting managers, but the implementation ultimately affected the whole organisation. The only way to get ownership of the implementation and results was to involve every employee.

The benefits so far have come from organisation and process change, those factors under the immediate control of people. Rank Xerox had successes and failures which were technology based, but most of the benefit obtained quickly has been process based, relatively low cost and durable. Ultimately, the new process must be supported by the right technologies; there is still a fear that the benefits will be eroded without the full foundation of process and technology support. It cannot ever be assumed that the end point has been reached.

Flexible implementation was critical. Every region of Europe had some freedom, not in the desired end point, but in the timing and way they achieved it.

It is not possible to over train or over communicate. Rank Xerox knew where it wanted to go but informing 20,000 people is a continuous process. Any improvement in communication forms the basis of the employee expectation for the future. Constant feedback and improvement are vital. A simple example is the increasing trend to work away from a permanent office base. People like the freedom this gives, but lose contact with routine communication meetings. Rank Xerox has introduced cassette and video tapes that can be played in the car or at home, to help overcome this.

World-class productivity, in growth and output, depends on process improvement, people and empowerment with information linking them. Rank Xerox built on the solid basis of leadership through quality. This may not work for everybody but it was probably the only way recognised by Rank Xerox people, and appropriate for the culture. It is vital for Rank Xerox that productivity is at the top of the pyramid because while the visible product is document technology, copiers and printers, the intrinsic product is customer productivity. Customers are therefore always entitled to ask 'How does Rank Xerox itself achieve productivity?' The company itself has to be a convincing show-case for the full range of Rank Xerox products and services, using people, process management, information and technology to the best possible effect.

Royal Bank of Scotland – essential postscripts

Essentials for making it happen

In the final film in the *Star Wars* trilogy, *The Empire Strikes Back*, there was a moment when the hero Luke Skywalker went seeking a guru, someone who could help him become a true Jedi knight and all that went with it – insight, intelligence, wisdom, compassion and an ability to conquer evil. Our hero met his unlikely guru Joda whose primary piece of advice was that, if Luke was to succeed in his quest, 'you have to believe – you need to have a vision'.

If there was a guru of change management, they would probably offer similar advice. Successful and impactful change has to be led, in doing so the leader has to put themselves at risk. This is precisely what managing director Schofield did. If Glasgow had been an abysmal failure, his illustrious career would probably have ended in ignominy.

There also has to be a well thought and thorough basic design methodology. This is what McKinsey brought to the party. However, the design methodology has to be flexible enough to cope with unexpected shifts and changes. It also helps if there is a healthy degree of scepticism, so don't shoot all the Jonahs; they play a valuable role in questioning the basic assumption – if they can't be convinced of what you propose, then you probably shouldn't be doing it.

We found that being explicit in defining the organisation proposition to its staff is critical. Failure to do so will increase resistance and ultimately the risk of another technically sound programme not reaping the projected benefits.

Phased implementation, where possible, allows learning to take place that ensures mistakes are not compounded. Implementation has to be carried out by those who are going to operate the systems. A valuable lesson learnt from the Royal Bank of Scotland's experience is they cannot be brought on board early enough. The new leaders have to be relieved of their current duties and allowed to immerse themselves in the new challenge.

Communications have to be of the highest quality framed in language and style of those to whom it is aimed. Hold focus groups regularly to test ideas, concepts and thinking and never be afraid to learn from the most unexpected sources. While the content and concept of the *New roles* brochure was developed by HR, the style of presentation and the breadth of content was heavily influenced by junior staff as a result of focus group discussions.

Benchmarking of practice and process played an important part of what was done. However, all too often benchmarking descends into industrial tourism. For benchmarking to be of any value, it has to be focused and clear agendas have to be set. However, most important of all, before starting out the benchmarker has to have a reasonably well-developed idea of what they are intending to do, as copying someone else's practice is not a recipe for success. Benchmarking can only help refine thinking, it does not replace it.

In any change programme there are likely to be casualties. Treat these people extremely well, be fair and compassionate, as those who remain will look to this group for indications as to how the future is to be. An early decision taken prior to rolling out the change programme in earnest was to introduce an employee assistance programme (EAP). The EAP was primarily designed as an outlet for those who were to remain. It is essentially a confidential counselling service, available 24 hours per day, 365 days per year to all staff and their immediate families. Interestingly enough, the majority of calls during the first year were from families and usually not connected to issues as a result of the change programme.

The implementation timetable has to be aggressive and demanding – almost unreasonable. Failure to do so will allow those in favour of the *status quo* to hold sway.

What would be done differently

The sense of ownership developed by the business initiative teams meant that in some cases they were reluctant to let go. As a consequence, some of the redesigned processes were initially suboptimally implemented, as the new line managers didn't feel enough ownership and in some cases felt disempowered. This sent out contradictory messages that conflicted dramatically with the whole concept of the change programme. Furthermore, by only giving the new line managers the process, they had few of the tools, motivation or understanding to instigate and manage change on a continuous basis. Furthermore, if the process had faults, rarely did the new leadership group have sufficient ownership for rectification; consequently 'not invented here' became a common cry.

Compromises are always going to happen; however, one area where they cannot be allowed is in selection. Whether internal or external, who is put into key roles is the most visible manifestation of change. Compromises here undermine valuable work being done elsewhere.

In the case of the Royal Bank of Scotland, much of the learning, training and development design could not take place until jobs had been tested in the field. In spite of this, a dedicated development team has to be put in place at an early stage in the process redesign work. As a result of the development team coming late to the party, they were asked to run a marathon on a middle distance runner's training – possible but painful.

Implementation is at the core. First of all it has to be owned. Second, there is a huge body of research that can inform, particularly on the human side of re-engineering. However, rarely will this research be found in the 'popular' management texts. Nevertheless, many of those who are leading elements of change programmes will treat the 'popular' texts as their bible. For those charged with defining the processes, it is clear from experience gained in the Royal Bank of Scotland that having a clear architecture for the core HR processes was critical. Equally important was having an underlying body of empirical research that could justify why 'popular' models, ideas and concepts were inappropriate.

We found that leading change is a lonely and at times painful experience. The impact on the leaders can be profound, particularly as they have few people around them with whom they can discuss things. There is a case for identifying suitable external mentors, individuals of experience to whom the leader may go, to use as a sounding board, coach and counsellor.

Toshiba – essential postscripts

In terms of making it happen, Toshiba probably had no alternative. The need for sweeping change was a 'given' to survival. The time-scale involved, which was only six months, in order to plan, design and implement, required a concentration of effort of a considerable kind. This was an unusual process; we had no opportunity to test and validate as we went; there were no pilots. We could only do our best with the best people that we could find at the time.

The imperatives of continuing to supply television products in the European market-place probably encouraged the ultimate holding company in Japan to accept a higher level of risk than would have been the case had there been the kind of time available that would be normally involved in a project of that dimension. It can only be conjecture whether or not the outcomes would have been better. It is almost certain they would have been different but the parent was in no position to recommend alternative strategies. The scene was not entirely unknown for the parent company. All of the top team involved were 'known quantities' and each of them was highly regarded. Nevertheless, it probably took top-down direction from the President of Toshiba Corporation for the green light to be given.

We didn't know for certain that what we were designing was going to be optimal but our collective views and experience suggested that, if consistently applied and if all sides honoured their agreement (management, union and parent company), there was at least a good chance of success or even better. At least we had faith in ourselves.

The approach that the team adopted of a 'blank page', starting from base, was that proposals being earnestly debated brought forth new and creative ideas from all of the team members.

Many things we could have done better. Much more training for everybody but particularly for management and supervisors. Time constrained the amount of training that could be done, but more training for entirely new roles and sensitivities would have avoided or reduced some of the difficulties that were experienced in the early stages. More time in finalising and improving implementation processes would have been welcomed but could, in the particular circumstances, just not have been made available.

For most involved, the conclusion is that, given the chance again, the same design outcomes would be proposed. It would have been harder to communicate more at the outset than was done but the pressures of growth and moving away from the euphoria of the start-up led to regression in communication standards by some. Better monitoring during the first year could have helped identify this.

The ultimate proof of the pudding, it can be said, lies not in the eating but in the digestion. In that regard, the sea-change initiatives adopted at the start still provide the foundations for the present-day operations. They also provide a viable framework for change initiatives probably yet to come.

Formidable realities

The first formidable reality to understand and accept, is that for successful delivery of the fundamental, widespread, and sweeping change that characterises BPR with ongoing efficiency, beyond implementation, all human resource support systems will need to change. But it is *attitudes*, not support systems, that are the vital ingredients that make the difference.

Understanding *why* behaviours in an organisation need to change and *how* they can and will be changed, is as much a challenge to BPR architects' own behaviours, as it is for them to bring about wider understanding, acceptance and action.

Some very relevant conclusions from other studies are:

> ... it is not so much human resource policies in general that have an impact on performance but a specific type of human resource approach that offers distinct advantages ... where the personnel/HR policies are integrated into a coherent philosophy and where this fits the business strategy, then superior performance results.[53]

> ... employee skills, abilities and competencies are seen to be sources of competitive advantage ... the personnel function's contribution to the development of these competencies is perceived at the 'tactical' level of recruitment, training and development practices.[54]

For an organisation to deliver and sustain effective business process re-engineering, the human resource management function must change or be changed.

Contribution is required of highly skilled and knowledgeable human resource 'engineers' to make informed strategic contributions, as well as 'technicians' and 'mechanics' to deliver tactical solutions. HR engineers need high level business/operational understanding as well as specialist knowledge.

Re-engineering the HR function(s) is an integral part of business process re-engineering.

Human resource practitioners will (hopefully) never be the same again.

REFERENCES AND NOTES

1 CSC INDEX. *State of Reengineering* (Report), CSC Index, 1994.

2 GRINT, K. and WILLCOCKS, L. 'Business Process Re-engineering in Theory and Practice: Business Paradise Regained?', *New Technology, Work and Employment*, 10,2, 1995.

3 HAMMER, M. 'Reengineering Work: Don't Automate, Obliterate', *Harvard Business Review*, July–August, 1990, pp. 104–112.

4 HAMMER, M. and CHAMPY, J. *Reengineering the Corporation, A Manifesto for Business Revolution*, New York, Harper Business, 1993.

5 WELLINS, R.S. and MURPHY, J.S. 'Reengineering: Plug Into the Human Factor', USA, *Training and Development*, January, 1995, pp. 30–35 (p.33).

6 KAPLAN, R.G. and MURDOCK, L. 'Core Process Redesign', *The McKinsey Quarterly*, No. 2, 1991, pp. 27–43.

7 HARVEY, D. *Reengineering: the Critical Success Factors*, London, Business Intelligence, 1994 (2nd edn published 1995).

8 CARR, D.K. and JOHANSSON, I.J. *Best Practices in Reengineering, What Works and What Doesn't in the Reengineering Process*, New York, McGraw-Hill, 1995, p. 17.

9 HAMMER and CHAMPY (1993), *op. cit.*

10 CARR and JOHANSSON (1995), *op. cit.*

11 HARVEY (1994), *op. cit.*

12 CSC INDEX (1994), *op. cit.*

13 GRINT and WILLCOCKS (1995), *op. cit.*

14 LEWIS, M. with other members of the planning team for this book. Planning meeting 31 January 1995.

15 WILLCOCKS, L. and SMITH, G. 'IT-Enabled Business Process Reengineering: Organisational and Human Resource Dimensions', *Journal of Strategic Information Systems*, 4,3, 1995.

16 WILLMOTT, H. 'Business Process Re-engineering and Human Resource Management', *Personnel Review*, Vol. 23, No. 3, 1994, pp. 34–46 (p. 40).

17 HAMMER, M. (1990), *op. cit.*, p. 107.

18 LOWENTHAL, J.N. 'Reengineering the Organization: A Step-by-Step Approach to Corporate Revitalization', *Quality Progress*, January/March, 1994, pp. 416–430 (p. 424).

19 HALL, G., ROSENTHAL, J. and WADE, J. 'How to Make Reengineering Really Work', *Harvard Business Review*, January–December, 1993, pp. 119–130.

20 GOSS, T., PASCALE, R. and ATHOS, A. 'The Reinvention Roller Coaster: Risking the Present for a Powerful Future', *Harvard Business Review*, November–December, 1993, pp. 98–108 (p. 99).

21 HOWARD, A. and WELLINS, R. *High-involvement Leadership, Changing Roles for Changing Times*, Pittsburgh PA, Development Dimensions International, Leadership Research Institute, 1994, pp. 11–12.

22 STRASSMANN, P.A. 'The Hocus Pocus of Reengineering', *The Quality Yearbook* (USA), 1994, pp. 431–436.

23 Harvey (1994), *op. cit.*

24 *Ibid.*

25 WELLINS, R.S., BYHAM, W.C. and DIXON, G.R., *Inside Teams – How 20 World-class Organizations are Winning Through Teamwork*, San Francisco, Jossey-Bass Publishers, 1994, p. 3.

26 LOWENTHAL, J.N. (1994), op. cit., p. 427.

27 WELLINS (1995), *op. cit.*, p. 35.

28 LAWLER, E.E. 'Effective Reward Systems: Strategy, Diagnosis, and Design', *Diagnosis for Organizational Change*, New York, The Guilford Press, 1994, pp. 210–238 (p. 211).

29 *Ibid.*

30 KELLY, J. and GENNARD, J. *The Role of Personnel Directors on the Board of Directors*, Glasgow, Strathclyde University Business School, unpublished paper, 1994.

31 ANSOFF, H.I. *Implanting Strategic Management*, Hemel Hempstead, Prentice Hall, 1984.

32 HAMMER (1990), *op. cit.*, p. 105.

33 HOFSTEDE, G. *Cultures and Organisations – Software of the Mind*, Maidenhead, McGraw-Hill, 1991.

34 HARVEY (1994), *op. cit.*

35 LEWIN, K. 'Frontiers in group dynamics', *Human Relations*, 1947.

36 ANSOFF (1984), *op. cit.*

37 OBOLENSKY, N. *Practical Business Re-engineering – Tools and Techniques for Achieving Effective Change*, London, Kogan Page, 1994, p. 292.

38 TREVOR, M. *Toshiba's New British Company – Competitiveness Through Innovation in Industry*, London, Policy Studies Institute, 1988.

39 ANSOFF (1984), *op. cit.*

40 BEER, S. *Diagnosing the System – For Organisations*, John Wiley & Sons, 1985.

41 INSTITUTE OF PERSONNEL AND DEVELOPMENT. *The IPD Guide on Occupational Health and Organisational Effectiveness*, London, Institute of Personnel and Development, 1995.

42 MAYO, E. *The Human Problems of Civilization*, Macmillan, 1933. (Mayo identified that people had complex needs, satisfied through informal social processes. One implication was that people tend to try harder when they feel the spotlight is on them.)

43 ORAM, M. *Japanese In-company Learning*, London, National Commission on Education, New Series Briefing No. 4, April 1995.

44 HANDY, C. 'Trust and the Virtual Organisation – How Do You Manage People Whom You Do Not See?', *Harvard Business Review*, May–June, 1995, pp. 40–50.

45 ANDREWS, G. 'Mistrust: The Hidden Obstacle to Empowerment', *HR Magazine*, Vol. 39, No. 9, US Society for Human Resource Management, 1994.

46 HOWARD and WELLINS (1994), *op. cit.*

47 WILSON, M., GEORGE, J. and WELLINS, R.S. with BYHAM, W.C. *Leadership Trapeze – Strategies for Leadership in Team-based Organizations*, San Francisco, Jossey-Bass Publishers, 1994, pp. 6–16.

48 FRANCIS, D. *Unblocking Organisation Communication*, Aldershot, Gower, 1987.

49 WELLINS, R.S., BYHAM, W.C. and WILSON, J.M. *Empowered Teams – Creating Self-directed Work Groups That Improve Quality, Productivity and Participation*, San Francisco, Jossey-Bass Publishers, 1991.

50 MAYO, E. *The Social Problems of an Industrial Civilisation*, Routledge & Kegan Paul, 1949.

51 DUNN, S. 'From Donovan to ... wherever', *British Jounal of Industrial Relations*, Vol. 31, No. 2, 1993. (The Donovan Commission was a Royal Commission on Trade Unions and Employers' Associations, which published its report in 1968.)

52 MARCHINGTON, M., WILKINSON, A., ACKERS, P. and GOODMAN, J. 'The Influence of Managerial Relations on Waves of Employee Involvement', *British Journal of Industrial Relations*, December, 1993, pp. 553–576.

53 GUEST, D and HOQUE, K. 'Personnel Management and Performance', in *The Contribution of Personnel Management to Organisational Performance*, London, Institute of Personnel and Development, Issues in People Management, Report No. 9, 1995, p. 8.

54 TYSON, S., DOHERTY, N. and VINEY, C. 'The Contribution of Personnel Management to Business Performance', in *The Contribution of Personnel Management to Organisational Performance*, London, Institute of Personnel and Development, Issues in People Management, Report No. 9, 1995, p. 35.

BIBLIOGRAPHY

Andrews, G. 'Mistrust: The Hidden Obstacle to Empowerment', *HR Magazine*, Vol. 39, No. 9, US Society for Human Resource Management, 1995.

Ansoff, H.I. *Implanting Strategic Management*, Hemel Hempstead, Prentice Hall, 1984.

Bashein, B.J., Markus, M.L. and Riley, P. 'Preconditions for BPR Success – And How to Prevent Failures', *Information Systems Management*, Spring, 1994, pp. 7–13.

Beardwell, I. and Holden, L. (Eds.) *Human Resource Management: A Contemporary Perspective*, London, Pitman Publishing, 1994.

Beer, S. *Diagnosing the System for Organisations*, Chichester, John Wiley & Sons, 1985.

Blyton, P. and Turnbull, P. *Reassessing Human Resource Management*, London, Sage, 1992.

Bramham, J. *Human Resource Planning*, London, Institute of Personnel and Development, (2nd Edn), 1994.

Burke, G. and Peppard, J. *Examining Business Process Re-engineering: Current Perspectives and Research Directions*, London, Cranfield Management Series, Kogan Page, 1995.

Carr, D.K. and Johansson, I.J. *Best Practices in Reengineering, What Works and What Doesn't in the Reengineering Process*, New York, McGraw-Hill, 1995.

Crego, E.T., Jr. and Schiffrin, P.D. *Customer-Centered Reengineering, Remapping for Total Customer Values*, Burr Ridge, Illinois, Irwin, 1995.

CSC Index. *State of Reengineering (Report)*, CSC Index, 1994.

Davenport, T.H. *Process Innovation, Reengineering Work through Information Technology*, Boston, Harvard Business School Press, 1993.

Engeström, Y. *Training for Change: New Approach to Instruction in Working Life*, Geneva, International Labour Office, 1994.

Francis, D. *Unblocking Organisation Communication*, Aldershot, Gower, 1987.

Goss, T., Pascale, R. and Athos, A. 'The Reinvention Roller Coaster: Risking the Present for a Powerful Future', *Harvard Business Review*, November–December, 1993, pp. 98–108.

Grint, K. and Willcocks, L. 'Business Process Re-engineering in Theory and Practice: Business Paradise Regained?', *New Technology, Work and Employment*, 10,2, 1995.

Guest, D., Tyson, S., Doherty, N., Hoque, K. and Viney, C. *The Contribution of Personnel Management to Organisational Performance: Moving the Debate On*, London, Institute of Personnel and Development, Issues in People Management (Report), No. 9, 1995.

Hall, G., Rosenthall, J. and Wade, J. 'How to make Reengineering Really Work', *Harvard Business Review*, November–December, 1993, pp. 119–131.

Hammer, M. 'Reengineering Work: Don't Automate, Obliterate', *Harvard Business Review*, July–August, 1990, pp. 104–112.

Hammer, M. and Champy, J. *Reengineering the Corporation, A Manifesto for Business Revolution*, New York, Harper Business, 1993.

Hammer, M. and Stanton, S.A. *The Reengineering Revolution – A Handbook*, New York, HarperCollins, 1995.

Handy, C. 'Trust and the Virtual Organisation – How Do You Manage People Whom You Don't See?', *Harvard Business Review*, May–June, 1995, pp. 40–50.

Harrison, R. *Employee Development*, London, Institute of Personnel Management (now the Institute of Personnel and Development), 1992.

Harvey, D. *Reengineering: the Critical Success Factors*, London, Business Intelligence, 1994 (2nd Edn published 1995).

Hofstede, G. *Cultures and Organisations – Software of the*

Mind, Maidenhead, McGraw-Hill, 1991.

Howard, A. and Wellins, R. *High-involvement Leadership, Changing Roles for Changing Times*, Pittsburgh PA, Development Dimensions International, Leadership Research Institute, 1994.

Institute of Personnel and Development. *The IPD Guide on Occupational Health and Organisational Effectiveness*, London, Institute of Personnel and Development, 1995.

Kaplan, R.G. and Murdock, L. 'Core Process Redesign', *The McKinsey Quarterly*, No. 2, 1991, pp. 27–43

Kotter, J.P. 'Why Transformation Efforts Fail', *Harvard Business Review*, March–April, 1995, pp. 59–67.

Larkin, T.J and Larkin, S. *'Communicating Change – Winning Employee Support for New Business Goals*, New York, McGraw-Hill, 1994.

Lawler, E.E. 'Effective Reward Systems: Strategy, Diagnosis, and Design', *Diagnosis for Organizational Change*, New York, The Guilford Press, 1994.

Lewin, K. 'Frontiers in Group Dynamics', *Human Relations*, 1947.

Lowenthal, J.N. 'Reengineering the Organization: A Step-by-Step Approach to Corporate Revitalization', *Quality Progress*, January/March, 1994, pp. 416–430.

Marchington, M., *Managing the Team: A Guide to Successful Employee Involvement*, London, Blackwell, 1992.

Marchington, M., Goodman, J., Wilkinson, A. and Ackers, P. *New Developments in Employee Involvement*, Manchester School of Management (UMIST), Research Series No. 2, 1993.

Marchington, M., Wilkinson, A., Ackers, P. and Goodman, J. 'The Influence of Managerial Relations on Waves of Employee Involvement', *British Journal of Industrial Relations*, December, 1993, pp. 553–576.

Mayo, E. *The Human Problems of Civilization*, Macmillan, 1933.

Mayo, E. *The Social Problems of an Industrial Civilization*, Routledge & Kegan Paul, 1949.

Oblensky, N. *Practical Business Re-engineering – Tools and*

Techniques for Achieving Effective Change, London, Kogan Page, 1994.

Oram, M. *Change Tack!*, in G. Armstrong (Ed.) *View from the Bridge*, London, Institute of Personnel Management (now the Institute of Personnel and Development), 1993.

Oram, M. *Japanese In-company Learning*, London, National Commission on Education, New Series Briefing No. 4, April, 1995.

Peters, T.J. and Waterman, R.H. *In Search of Excellence - Lessons from America's Best-run Companies*, New York, Harper & Row, 1982.

Pettigrew, A. 'Longitudinal Field Research on Change: Theory and Practice', *Organisation Science*, No. 3, August, 1990.

Philips, N. *Innovative Management*, London, Pitman Publishing, 1993.

Prahalad, C.K. and Hamel, G. 'The Core Competencies of the Corporation', *Harvard Business Review*, May–June, 1990, pp. 79–89.

Senge, P. *The Fifth Discipline: The Art and Practice of the Learning Organisation*, Currency Doubleday, 1990.

Senge, P., Roberts, C., Ross, R.B., Smith, B.J. and Kleiner, A. *The Fifth Discipline Fieldbook: Strategies and Tools for Building a Learning Organisation*. London, Nicholas Brealey, 1994.

Simons, R. 'Control in an Age of Empowerment – How Can Managers Promote Innovation While Avoiding Unwelcome Surprises?', *Harvard Business Review*, March–April, 1995, pp. 80–88.

Strassmann, P.A. 'The Hocus Pocus of Reengineering', *The Quality Yearbook* (USA), 1994, pp. 431–436.

Taylor, J.C. and Felton, D.F. *Performance by Design – Sociotechnical Systems in North America*, New Jersey, Prentice Hall, 1993.

Trevor, M. *Toshiba's New British Company – Competitiveness Through Innovation in Industry*, London, Policy Studies Institute, 1988.

Wellins, R.S., Byham, W.C. and Dixon, G.R. *Inside Teams – How 20 World-class Organizations are Winning Through*

Teamwork, San Francisco, Jossey-Bass Publishers, 1994.

Wellins, R.S., Byham, W.C. and Wilson, J.M. *Empowered Teams - Creating Self-Directed Work Groups That Improve Quality, Productivity and Participation*, San Francisco, Jossey-Bass Publishers, 1991.

Wellins, R.S. and Murphy, J.S. 'Reengineering: Plug Into the Human Factor', USA, *Training and Development*, January, 1995, pp. 30–35.

Willcocks, L. and Smith, G. 'IT-Enabled Business Process Reengineering: Organizational and Human Resource Dimensions', *Journal of Strategic Information Systems*, 4,3, 1995.

Willmott, H. 'Business Process Re-engineering and Human Resource Management', *Personnel Review*, Vol.23, No. 3, 1994, pp. 34–46.

Wilson, M., George, J. and Wellins, R.S. with Byham, W.C. *Leadership Trapeze – Strategies for Leadership in Team-based Organizations*, San Francisco, Jossey-Bass Publishers, 1994.

INDEX